ADVCOMP 2017

The Eleventh International Conference on Advanced Engineering Computing and Applications in Sciences

November 12 - 16, 2017

Barcelona, Spain

ADVCOMP 2017 Editors

Claus-Peter Rückemann, Leibniz Universität Hannover / Westfälische Wilhelms-Universität Münster / North-German Supercomputing Alliance (HLRN), Germany

Dean Vucinic, Vesalius College/Vrije Universiteit Brussel, Belgium

Printed from e-media with permission by:

Curran Associates, Inc.
57 Morehouse Lane
Red Hook, NY 12571

Some format issues inherent in the e-media version may also appear in this print version.

Printed by Curran Associates, Inc. (2017)

International Academy, Research, and Industry Association (IARIA)
412 Derby Way
Wilmington, DE 19810

Phone: (408) 893-6407
Fax: (408) 527-6351

petre@iaria.org

Additional copies of this publication are available from:

Curran Associates, Inc.
57 Morehouse Lane
Red Hook, NY 12571 USA
Phone: 845-758-0400
Fax: 845-758-2633
Email: curran@proceedings.com
Web: www.proceedings.com

Table of Contents

ADVCOMP 2017

Forward

The Eleventh International Conference on Advanced Engineering Computing and Applications in Sciences (ADVCOMP 2017), held between November 12 - 16, 2017, in Barcelona, Spain, continued a series of events addressing fundamental advanced scientific computing and specific mechanisms and algorithms for particular sciences. The conference provided a forum where researchers were able to present recent research results and new research problems and directions related to them.

With the advent of high performance computing environments, virtualization, distributed and parallel computing, as well as the increasing memory, storage and computational power, processing particularly complex scientific applications and voluminous data is more affordable. With the current computing software, hardware and distributed platforms effective use of advanced computing techniques is more achievable.

With the advent of high performance computing environments, virtualization, distributed and parallel computing, as well as the increasing memory, storage and computational power, processing particularly complex scientific applications and voluminous data is more affordable. With the current computing software, hardware and distributed platforms effective use of advanced computing techniques is more achievable.

The event was very competitive in its selection process and very well perceived by the international scientific and industrial communities. As such, it has attracted excellent contributions and active participation from all over the world. We were very pleased to receive a large number of top quality contributions.

The conference had the following tracks:

- Computing applications in science
- Advances in computation methods
- Interdisciplinary computing
- Computing technologies

We take here the opportunity to warmly thank all the members of the ADVCOMP 2017 technical program committee, as well as all the reviewers. The creation of such a high quality conference program would not have been possible without their involvement. We also kindly thank all the authors that dedicated much of their time and effort to contribute to ADVCOMP 2017. We truly believe that, thanks to all these efforts, the final conference program consisted of top quality contributions.

We also gratefully thank the members of the ADVCOMP 2017 organizing committee for their help in handling the logistics and for their work that made this professional meeting a success.

We hope that ADVCOMP 2017 was a successful international forum for the exchange of ideas and results between academia and industry and to promote further progress in the field of advanced engineering computing and applications. We also hope that Barcelona, Spain, provided a pleasant environment during the conference and everyone saved some time to enjoy the unique charm of the city.

ADVCOMP 2017 Chairs

ADVCOMP Steering Committee

Juha Röning, University of Oulu, Finland
Paul Humphreys, Ulster University, UK
Wasif Afzal, Mälardalen University, Sweden
Hans-Joachim Bungartz, TUM, Germany
Andreas Rausch, Technische Universität Clausthal, Germany
Ivan Rodero, Rutgers University - Piscataway, USA
Dean Vucinic, Vrije Universiteit Brussel (VUB), Belgium | FERIT, Croatia,
Wenbing Zhao, Cleveland State University, USA
Rudolf Berrendorf, Bonn-Rhein-Sieg University, Germany

ADVCOMP Industry/Research Advisory Committee

Yuri Alexeev, Argonne National Laboratory, USA
Marcin Hojny, AGH University of Science and Technology, Kraków, Poland
Alice Koniges, Lawrence Berkeley Laboratory/NERSC, USA
Marcin Paprzycki, Systems Research Institute, Polish Academy of Sciences, Poland
Folker Meyer, Argonne National Laboratory Computation Institute and Medical School | University of Chicago, USA
Jian Lin, Huawei Technologies Co. Ltd, Hangzhou, China
Simon Tsang, Vencore Labs Inc., USA
Alfred Geiger, T-Systems Solutions for Research GmbH, Germany
Hugo Daniel Meyer, University of Amsterdam, Netherlands

ADVCOMP 2017
Committee

ADVCOMP Steering Committee

Juha Röning, University of Oulu, Finland
Paul Humphreys, Ulster University, UK
Wasif Afzal, Mälardalen University, Sweden
Hans-Joachim Bungartz, TUM, Germany
Andreas Rausch, Technische Universität Clausthal, Germany
Ivan Rodero, Rutgers University - Piscataway, USA
Dean Vucinic, Vrije Universiteit Brussel (VUB), Belgium | FERIT, Croatia,
Wenbing Zhao, Cleveland State University, USA
Rudolf Berrendorf, Bonn-Rhein-Sieg University, Germany

ADVCOMP Industry/Research Advisory Committee

Yuri Alexeev, Argonne National Laboratory, USA
Marcin Hojny, AGH University of Science and Technology, Kraków, Poland
Alice Koniges, Lawrence Berkeley Laboratory/NERSC, USA
Marcin Paprzycki, Systems Research Institute, Polish Academy of Sciences, Poland
Folker Meyer, Argonne National Laboratory Computation Institute and Medical School | University of Chicago, USA
Jian Lin, Huawei Technologies Co. Ltd, Hangzhou, China
Simon Tsang, Vencore Labs Inc., USA
Alfred Geiger, T-Systems Solutions for Research GmbH, Germany
Hugo Daniel Meyer, University of Amsterdam, Netherlands

ADVCOMP 2017 Technical Program Committee

Wasif Afzal, Mälardalen University, Sweden
Ayaz Ahmad, COMSATS Institute of Information Technology, Pakistan
Francisco Airton Silva, Federal University of Piauí, Brazil
Yuri Alexeev, Argonne National Laboratory, USA
Sónia Maria Almeida da Luz, Polytechnic Institute of Leiria, Portugal
Daniel Andresen, Kansas State University, USA
Omar Andres Carmona Cortes, Instituto Federal do Maranhão, Brazil
Alberto Antonietti, Politecnico di Milano, Italy
Maha Arbi, University of Tunis (ISG-campus), Tunisia
Ehsan Atoofian, Lakehead University, Canada
Doo-Hwan Bae, School of Computing - KAIST, Korea
Jorge Barbosa, Universidade do Porto, Portugal
Carlos Becker Westphall, University of Santa Catarina, Brazil

R. Ben Djemaa, Institut Supérieur d'Informatique et des Techniques de Communication, Tunisia
Rudolf Berrendorf, Bonn-Rhein-Sieg University, Germany
Md Zakirul Alam Bhuiyan, Fordham University, USA
Muhammad Naufal Bin Mansor, University Malaysia Perlis, Malaysia
Kai Bu, Zhejiang University, China
Hans-Joachim Bungartz, TUM, Germany
Maxwell Cai, Leiden University, Netherlands
Xiao-Chuan Cai, University of Colorado Boulder, USA
Laura Carrington, PMaC Labs - SDSC/UCSD / EP Analytic Inc., USA
Mete Celik, Erciyes University, Turkey
Hsi-Ya Chang, National Center for High-performance Computing, Taiwan
Huangke Chen. National University of Defense Technology, China
Christian Contarino, University of Trento, Italy
Juan Manuel Corchado Rodríguez, University of Salamanca, Spain
Andrews Cordolino Sobral, University of La Rochelle, France
Gianpiero Costantino, IIT - CNR, Italy
Marisa da Silva Maximiano, Polytechnic of Leiria, Portugal
Marcelo de Paiva Guimarães, Federal University of São Paulo, Brazil
Vassilios V. Dimakopoulos, University of Ioannina, Greece
Mahdi Esfahanian, Florida Atlantic University, USA
Javier Fabra, Universidad de Zaragoza, Spain
Tiziano Fagni, Institute of Informatics and Telematics (IIT) - CNR, Pisa, Italy
Ali Farhadi, University of Memphis, USA
Akemi Galvez Tomida, University of Cantabria, Spain
Marc Gamell, Intel Corporation, USA
Félix J. García Clemente, University of Murcia, Spain
Leonardo Garrido, Tecnológico de Monterrey, Mexico
Filippo Gaudenzi, Università degli Studi di Milano, Italy
Alfred Geiger, T-Systems Solutions for Research GmbH, Germany
J. Paul Gibson, Telecom Sud Paris, France
Teofilo Gonzalez, University of California Santa Barbara, USA
Bernard Grabot, LGP-ENIT, France
Jagadeesh Gunda, University of Edinburgh, UK
Yanfei Guo, MCS Division | ANL, USA
Maki Habib, American University in Cairo, Egypt
Shaza Hanif, Higher Colleges of Technology, Sharjah, United Arab Emirates
Houcine Hassan, Universidad Politécnica de Valencia, Spain
Mohd Helmy Abd Wahab, Universiti Tun Hussein Onn Malaysia, Malaysia
Marcin Hojny, AGH University of Science and Technology, Kraków, Poland
Wladyslaw Homenda, Warsaw University of Technology, Poland
Tzung-Pei Hong, National University of Kaohsiung, Taiwan
Michael Hübner, Ruhr-University of Bochum, Germany
Paul Humphreys, Ulster University, UK

Andres Iglesias, University of Cantabria, Spain / Toho University, Japan
Joanna Isabelle Olszewska, University of Gloucestershire, UK
Mohamed Ismail, University of Regina, Canada
Koteswar Rao Jerripothula, Nanyang Technological University, Singapore
Eugene John, The University of Texas at San Antonio, USA
Jie Kong, Xi'an Shiyou University, China
Alice Koniges, Lawrence Berkeley Laboratory/NERSC, USA
Harald Köstler, Friedrich-Alexander University Erlangen-Nürnberg, Germany
Pan Lai, Nanyang Technological University, Singapore
Seyong Lee, Oak Ridge National Laboratory, USA
Maurizio Leotta, University of Genova, Italy
Clement Leung, Hong Kong Baptist University - United International College, Hong Kong
Yiu-Wing Leung, Hong Kong Baptist University, Kowloon Tong, Hong Kong
Jiajia Li, Georgia Institute of Technology, USA
Jian Li, University of Massachusetts Amherst, USA
Jian Lin, Huawei Technologies Co. Ltd, Hangzhou, China
Chin-Jung Liu, Michigan State University, USA
Xiaoyi Lu, The Ohio State University, USA
Emilio Luque, University Autonoma of Barcelona (UAB), Spain
Stephane Maag, Telecom SudParis, France
Elbert E. N. Macau, Instituto Nacional de Pesquisas Espaciais – INPE, Brazil
Parikshit Maini, IIIT-Delhi, India
Shikharesh Majumdar, Carleton University, Canada
Laci Mary Manhães, Public University of Navarre, Spain
Claudia Marcos, ISISTAN Research Institute | UNICEN University, Argentina
Marcin Markowski, Wroclaw University of Science and Technology, Poland
Alessandro Margara, Politecnico di Milano, Italy
Cleyton Mário de Oliveira Rodrigues, University of Pernambuco, Brazil
Piyush Mehrotra, NASA Ames Research Center, USA
Folker Meyer, Argonne National Laboratory Computation Institute and Medical School | University of Chicago, USA
Hugo Daniel Meyer, University of Amsterdam, Netherlands
Mariofanna Milanova, University of Arkansas at Little Rock, USA
Subrata Mitra, Adobe Research, India
Ilya Moiseenko, Cisco Systems, USA
Sébastien Monnet, University Savoie Mont Blanc, France
Elena Maria Navarro Martinez, Universidad de Castilla-La Mancha, Spain
Sarah Odofin, Northumbria University, UK
Marcin Paprzycki, Systems Research Institute, Polish Academy of Sciences, Poland
Prantosh Kumar Paul, Raiganj University, India
Sumit Purohit, Pacific Northwest National Laboratory, USA
Andreas Rausch, Technische Universität Clausthal, Germany
Michael M. Resch, University of Stuttgart, Germany
Diego P. Ruiz, University of Granada, Spain

Thanasis Papaioannou, Athens University of Economics and Business (AUEB), Greece
Kwangjin Park, Wonkwang University, South Korea
Sonia Pérez Díaz, University of Alcala, Spain
Radu-Emil Precup, Politehnica University of Timisoara, Romania
Vaibhav Rastogi, University of Wisconsin, USA
Javed Razzaq, Bonn-Rhein-Sieg University of Applied Sciences, Germany
Barbara Re, University of Camerino, Italy
Carlos Reaño, Technical University of Valencia, Spain
Michele Risi, University of Salerno,Italy
Ivan Rodero, Rutgers University - Piscataway, USA
Juha Röning, University of Oulu, Finland
Swarup Roy, North-Eastern Hill University, India
Julio Sahuquillo, Universitat Politecnica de Valencia, Spain
Subhash Saini, NASA, USA
Sebastiano Fabio Schifano, Universita' di Ferrara, Italy
Erich Schweighofer, University of Vienna, Austria
Alireza Shahrabi, Glasgow Caledonian University, UK
Justin Y. Shi, Temple University, USA
Neha Shreya, Indian Institute of Tourism and Travel management, Noida, India
Min Si, Argonne National Laboratory, USA
Francesco Spegni, Universita` Politecnica delle Marche, Italy
Giandomenico Spezzano, ICAR-CNR | University of Calabria, Italy
Emanuele Storti, Università Politecnica delle Marche, Italy
Yulei Sui, University of New South Wales (UNSW), Australia
Yifan Sun, Technicolor Research, Los Altos, California
Gabriel Tanase, IBM TJ Watson Research Center, USA
Andrei Tchernykh, CICESE Research Center, Mexico
Priscila Tiemi Maeda Saito, Federal University of Technology - Paraná (UTFPR-CP), Brazil
QuocNam Tran, The University of South Dakota, USA
Simon Tsang, Vencore Labs Inc., USA
Costas Vassilakis, University of the Peloponnese, Greece
Adriano Velasque Werhli, Universidade Federal do Rio Grande - FURG, Brazil
Juan Vicente Capella Hernández, Universitat Politècnica de València, Spain
Dario Vieira, EFREI, France
Konstantinos Votis, Information Technologies Institute | Centre for Research and Technology Hellas, Thessaloniki, Greece
Dean Vucinic, Vrije Universiteit Brussel (VUB), Belgium | FERIT, Croatia
Guodong Wang, South Dakota School of Mines and Technology, USA
Yunsheng Wang, Kettering University, USA
Gabriel Wittum, Goethe University Frankfurt, Germany
Hui Wu, The University of New South Wales, Australia
Mudasser F. Wyne, National University, USA
Qiao Xiang, Yale University, USA
Cong-Cong Xing, Nicholls State University, USA

Zhijie Xu, University of Huddersfield, UK
Reda Yaich, Institut Mines-Télécom, France
Xu Yang, Illinois Institute of Technology, Chicago, USA
Yingzhen Yang, Snap Research, Australia
Quan Yuan, University of Texas of the Permian Basin, USA
Vesna Zeljkovic, Lincoln University, USA
Jianping Zeng, University of Nebraska-Lincoln, USA
Na Zhang, VMware Inc., USA
Wenbing Zhao, Cleveland State University, USA
Peter Ziegenhein, The Institute of Cancer Research / The Royal Marsden NHS Foundation Trust, London, UK

A Second-Order Regularization Method of Object Reconstruction in Hydrodynamic Experiments

LingHai Kong, HaiBo Xu
Institute of Applied Physics and Computational Mathematics
Beijing, PR China
email: {kong_linghai, xu_haibo) @iapcm.ac.cn

***Abstract*— A new higher-order regularization model is investigated under the assumption of mixed Laplace-Gaussian noise, which plays an important role in tomography reconstruction and quantitative analysis of hydrodynamic experiments. To solve the model numerically, adaptive stopping functions are introduced to improve the classical augmented Lagrangian method, and an adaptive soft-shrinking formula is derived. To acquire efficiency and reliability, it is further combined with a variant of the expectation maximization method. Some experimental tests are performed for image denoising and object reconstruction.**

Keywords- Regularization Method; Mixed Laplace-Gaussian Noise; ALM; EM;Image Reconstruction.

I. Introduction

Image reconstruction is an indispensable process in image processing and data analysis, whose goal is to rebuild an ideal image from noisy or even blurred data. Some different types of mixed noise models have been investigated in the literature, such as Poisson and Gaussian noise [1][2], impulse and Gaussian noise [3]-[5], etc.. With regards to impulse noise, two special cases have drawn much research interest, that is, salt-and-pepper noise and random-valued noise. Nevertheless, in some applications, such as harsh hydrodynamic experiments, additive white Gaussian noise is introduced as expected during image acquisition, while non-Gaussian noise, especially additive Laplace noise, is also encountered for more accurate modeling transmission in Charge-coupled Device (CCD) channels and interaction between shielding and photons. Accordingly, this paper considers the task of removing mixed Laplace-Gaussian (MLG) noise, where the observation f of an ideal image u is modeled by

$$f(x) = Hu(x) + n(x), x \in U$$

U denotes the image domain, $n(x)$ is regarded as a realization of independent and identically distributed (iid) random variables $Z(x)$, which has the probability density function (PDF)

$$p_Z(z;\theta) = \sum_{k=1}^{2} \gamma_k p_k(z;\sigma_k^2), \quad (1)$$

where

$$p_1(z;\sigma_1^2) = \frac{1}{2\sigma_1^2}\exp(-|z|/\sigma_1^2),$$

$$p_2(z;\sigma_2^2) = \frac{1}{\sqrt{2\pi\sigma_2^2}}\exp(-|z|^2/2\sigma_2^2)$$

$\theta = \{\theta_1, \theta_2\} = \{\gamma_i, \sigma_i^2, i = 1,2\}$ is a parameter set, $\gamma_i > 0$ represents the mixture ratio satisfying $\gamma_1 + \gamma_2 = 1$. Additionally, H can be an identity, blur or projection operator in this paper. The problem of this paper is then to reconstruct u from the observation f with an unknown parameter set $\boldsymbol{\theta}$.

The First-Order Total Variation (FOTV) regularization method, designed originally for Gaussian noise removal, is now one of the most popular approaches for studying inverse problems under various assumptions of noise including Poisson, Speckle, impulse, or even mixed noise. Among the works in the literature, the first-order regularization models given in [6]-[8] are of benefit to our work.

Given the success of FOTV-based models, various modifications have been developed to surmount its artifact, such as the staircase effect and the shortage of smoothness. Among the modifications, we concentrate on the following Higher-Order TV (HOTV) regularization methods. Li, Shen, Fan, Shen [9] proposed the following model

$$\min_u \int_U \left((1-g)|\nabla u| + g|\nabla u|^2\right)dx + \frac{\beta}{2}\int_U (u-f)^2 dx \quad (2)$$

for Gaussian noise removal, where g is a stopping function producing anisotropic diffusion and a weighted fourth-order diffusion equation is derived by steepest descent method. Papafitsoros and Shcönlieb [10] considered the Gauss noise model and the impulse noise model separately, and established a theoretical and numerical framework of the minimization problem

$$\min_u \int_U \left(\alpha \mathrm{a}(\nabla u) + \beta \mathrm{b}(|\nabla u|^2)\right)dx + \frac{1}{s}\int_U (Tu - \mathrm{f})^2 dx \quad (3)$$

where s=1,2, T is a known linear operator, $\alpha \geq 0, \beta \geq 0$ are regularization parameters, and the convex functions $\mathrm{a}(\cdot), \mathrm{b}(\cdot)$ have at most linear growth at infinity. They also assured that, by implementing a higher order extension of FOTV, the proposed model can significantly reduce the staircase effect in image restoration.

As mentioned above, the primary goal of this paper is to find an appropriate model for mixed noise removal and image reconstruction. Most existing regularization models have the data fidelity terms determined by the probability distributions of the noises, such as L^2 norm for Gaussian noise and L^1 norm for impulse noise. In applications, however, it is still not well-founded for the noise model, as well as higher-order regularization methods used for hydro-dynamic experiments, since the parameters of the PDF are unknown in advance and has to be considered carefully. Moreover, it is not unnecessary to reconsider the assemblage of the punishing functions, and the weighting functions should have been investigated in a more natural and practical way. In view of that, the problem of image reconstruction is reconsidered and a new framework of the second order regularization method is proposed. Noting that noise modeling is indispensable for image processing and data diagnosing, the first main contribution of this paper is to introduce an applicable calculation method for the parameters of the PDF, which can be generalized to more intricate simulations of real noise. The second contribution lies in designing an efficient and reliable Augmented Lagrange Method (ALM) to solve a constrained minimization problem, where some kind of positive control functions are designed to enhance significant details. The numerical discussion confirms that the proposed model succeeds in avoiding the undesirable pseudo-features in the reconstructed data.

The rest of the paper is organized as follows. In section 2, applying Bayesian inference theory, a new hybrid regularization model is proposed. Furthermore, its algorithm is established with some modification of the ALM. In section 3, some numerical experiments are conducted to prove the applicability of the proposed models. Finally, in section 4, some additional remarks and future work on the model and its algorithm are discussed.

II. MAIN MODEL AND ITS ALGORITHM

A. Mathematical Modeling

The main idea is to configure a regularization model by combing FOTV functionals with HOTV ones through some kinds of weighting functions, intending to enhance true edges and polish fake or insignificant information in the reconstructed images.

By applying the Bayesian inference theory [11] in continuous settings, the maximum a-posteriori probability (MAP) estimator of u is given by

$$u^{*} = \mathrm{argmin}_{u}\left\{-\int_U \ln p(f|u)\mathrm{dx} - \int_U \ln p(u)\mathrm{dx}\right\} \quad (4)$$

It follows from the ideas in [10] that the a priori probability density function, $p(u)$, can be defined by

$$p(u) \sim \exp\left(-\mathrm{R}(\nabla u, \nabla^2 u)\right)$$

$$\mathrm{R}(\nabla u, \nabla^2 u) = -\int_U (\alpha|\nabla u| + \tau|\nabla^2 u|)\mathrm{dx}, \quad (5)$$

where α, τ are positive parameters. On the other hand, by the independency assumption, there holds that

$$p(f|u) = p_Z(f - Hu; \theta).$$

We then have a negative log-likelihood functional of the MLG model

$$L(\theta, u) =$$

$$-\int_U \left(\ln\left[\frac{\gamma_1}{2\sigma_1^2}\exp\left(-\frac{|f-Hu|}{\sigma_1^2}\right)\right] + \ln\left[\frac{\gamma_2}{\sqrt{2\pi\sigma_2^2}}\exp\left(-\frac{|f-Hu|^2}{2\sigma_2^2}\right)\right]\right)\mathrm{dx} \quad (6)$$

The difficulty of computing the minimizer of the functional (6) lies in the log-sum operation. Fortunately, it can be surmounted in the following way. Introduce a vector-valued function $\varphi = \{\varphi_1, \varphi_2\}$ [4], [12] in

$$\Delta_+ = \{\varphi(\mathrm{x}) | 0 < \varphi_i(\mathrm{x}) < 1, \textstyle\sum_{i=1}^{2} \varphi_i(\mathrm{x}) = 1\},$$

and define a functional

$$\aleph(\theta, u, \varphi) =$$

$$\int_U \sum_{i=1}^{2} \varphi_i(\mathrm{x})[P_i(\mathrm{x}) - \ln Q(\mathrm{x})]\mathrm{dx} + \int_U \sum_{i=1}^{2} \varphi_i \ln \varphi_i \,\mathrm{dx} \quad (7)$$

where

$$P_1(\mathrm{x}) = \frac{|Hu-f|}{\sigma_1^2}, P_2(\mathrm{x}) = \frac{|Hu-f|^2}{2\sigma_2^2},$$

$$Q_1(\mathrm{x}) = \frac{\gamma_1}{2\sigma_1^2}, Q_2(\mathrm{x}) = \frac{\gamma_2}{\sqrt{2\pi\sigma_2^2}}.$$

Then, perform the following iteration scheme

$$\begin{cases} \varphi^{v+1} = \mathrm{argmin}_{\varphi\in\Delta_+} \aleph(\theta^{v}, u^{v}, \varphi) \\ (\theta^{v+1}, u^{v+1}) = \mathrm{argmin}_{\theta,u} \aleph(\theta, u, \varphi^{v+1}) \end{cases} \quad (8)$$

for given θ^0, u^0, where v denotes the inner iteration number. Utilizing the updating equation

$$\varphi_i^{v+1} = \frac{\gamma_i p_i(Hu^{v} - f; \theta_i^{v})}{\sum_{s=1}^{2} \gamma_s^{v} p_s(Hu^{v} - f; \theta_s^{v})}, \mathrm{i} = 1,2 \quad (9)$$

it can be proven that the above scheme leads to the same global minimize of $L(\theta, u)$.

Thus, we turn to consider the following minimization problem (MLG-TVBH)

$$\min_{\theta,u} E(\theta, u) = \aleph(\theta, u, \varphi^{v+1}) + \mathrm{R}(\nabla u, \nabla^2 u). \quad (10)$$

B. Proposed algorithm of MLG-TVBH

The algorithm for MLG-TVBH is based on the variable splitting method and the ALM, where penalty parameters in the quadratic infeasibility terms of ALM are replaced by adaptively selective functions. Indeed, reuse the pattern of (8) and split (10) into several minimization sub-problems. Use v to detonate the iteration number. θ^0 is a coarse guess of the parameters θ , then the minimizer (θ^{v+1}, u^{v+1}) are given by

$$\begin{cases} u^{v+1} = \mathrm{argmin}_{u} E(\theta^{v}, u) \\ \theta^{v+1} = \mathrm{argmin}_{\theta} E(\theta, u^{v+1}) \end{cases} \quad (11)$$

iteratively.

In terms of calculating θ^{v+1}, it yields by direct computation that

$$(\sigma_1^2)^{v+1} = \frac{\int_U \varphi_1^{v+1}|Hu^{v+1} - f|\mathrm{dx}}{\int_U \varphi_1^{v+1}\mathrm{dx}}, (\sigma_2^2)^{v+1} = \frac{\int_U \varphi_2^{v+1}|Hu^{v+1} - f|^2\mathrm{dx}}{\int_U \varphi_2^{v+1}\mathrm{dx}}, \quad (12)$$

$$\gamma_1^{v+1} = \frac{\int_U \varphi_1^{v+1}\mathrm{dx}}{|U|}, \gamma_2^{v+1} = 1 - \gamma_1^{v+1}, |U| = \int_U 1\mathrm{dx} \quad (13)$$

As for the u-minimization problem of (11), it can be proven that there exists a unique solution in the space of bounded Hessian (BH) [10], the details of which are omitted in this paper.

To circumvent the non-differentiability of the L^1 norm arisen in our model, a modification of the Alternating Direction Augmented Lagrangian (ADAL) method [13][14] is proposed, as follows.

Firstly, introduce auxiliary vector-valued variables q, h, and split the minimization problem into

$$\min_{u,q,h} \aleph(\theta^{v}, u, \varphi^{v+1}) + \int_U (\alpha|q| + \tau|h|)\mathrm{dx} \text{ subject to } q = \nabla u, h = \nabla^2 u.$$

Secondly, configure an alternating minimization process. More specifically, use a third variable k to approximate the fidelity term $Hu - f$, and introduce spatially detail selective functions $\rho_k(\mathrm{x})$, $\rho_q(\mathrm{x})$, $\rho_h(\mathrm{x})$, and then consider the following functional

$$L^{\rho}(u, k, q, h; \mu) = \mathrm{S}(k) + \langle \mu_k, Hu - f - k\rangle + \int_U \alpha|q|\mathrm{dx} +$$

$$\frac{1}{2}\int_U \rho_k(x)|Hu-f-k|^2dx + \langle\mu_p,\nabla u - q\rangle + \frac{1}{2}\int_U \rho_q(x)|\nabla u - q|^2dx + \int_U \tau|h|dx + \langle\mu_h,\nabla^2 u - h\rangle + \frac{1}{2}\int_U \rho_h(x)|\nabla^2 u - h|^2dx$$

where $S(Hu-f) = \aleph(\theta^v, u, \varphi^{v+1}), \rho = (\rho_k, \rho_q, \rho_h)$ is the vector of positive penalty functions to be specified latter, $\mu = (\mu_k, \mu_q, \mu_h)$ is the vector of Lagrange multipliers.

Given initial values u^0, k^0, q^0, h^0. If u^v, k^v, q^v, h^v are the current approximation to the multiplier vector, the fidelity term, the gradient and the Hessian of the original data, then we turn to consider the following problems

$$\text{SP1}: u^{v+1} = \text{argmin}_u L^\rho(u, k^v, q^v, h^v; \mu^v) \quad (14)$$
$$\text{SP2}: k^{v+1} = \text{argmin}_k L^\rho(u^{v+1}, k, q^v, h^v; \mu^v) \quad (15)$$
$$\text{SP3}: q^{v+1} = \text{argmin}_q L^\rho(u^{v+1}, k^{v+1}, q, h^v; \mu^v) \quad (16)$$
$$\text{SP4}: h^{v+1} = \text{argmin}_h L^\rho(u^{v+1}, k^{v+1}, q^{v+1}, h; \mu^v) \quad (17)$$
$$\text{SP5}: \mu^{v+1} = \text{argmax}_\mu L^\rho(u^{v+1}, k^{v+1}, q^{v+1}, h^{v+1}; \mu) \quad (18)$$

For the minimization problem (14), which is a quadratic problem, by a routine computation, it yields the following fourth-order Euler-Lagrange equation

$$-\text{div}(\rho_q \nabla u) + \text{div}^2(\rho_h \nabla^2 u) + W(u,f) = 0 \quad (19)$$
$$W = \text{div}(\rho_q q^v - \mu_q) - \text{div}^2(\rho_h h^v - \mu_h) + H^*(\rho_k(Hu - f - k^v) + \mu_k^v) \quad (20)$$

with boundary conditions

$$\partial u/\partial N = \nabla u_x \cdot N = \nabla u_y \cdot N = 0$$
$$\langle \nabla\cdot(\rho_h \nabla u_x), n_1\rangle = \langle \nabla\cdot(\rho_h \nabla u_y), n_2\rangle = 0.$$

where $N = (n_1, n_2)$ is the outward unit normal vector to the boundary, H^* is the adjoint operator of H.

For the problem (15), combine it with the updating of μ_k in (18). Introduce an auxiliary variable m to approximate $Hu^{v+1} - f - k$, utilize the dual method, we find that the maximize μ_k^{v+1} fulfills

$$\frac{\mu_k^{v+1}}{\rho_k(x)} - \frac{\mu_k^v}{\rho_k(x)} = Hu^{v+1} - f - k^{v+1} \triangleq g.$$

Detonate $A(x) = \varphi_1^{v+1}/(\sigma_1^2)^v$, $B(x) = \varphi_2^{v+1}/(\sigma_2^2)^v$, consider $\delta M(k)/\delta k = 0$, where

$$M(k) = S(k) + \frac{1}{2}\int_U \rho_k\left(Hu^{v+1} - f - k + \frac{\mu_k^v}{\rho_k}\right)^2 dx,$$

there holds the following iteration scheme for solving (15):

$$\begin{cases} k^{v+1} = \frac{\rho_k}{B+\rho_k}\text{shrink}\left(g, \frac{\rho_k}{A}\right), \\ \frac{\mu_k^{v+1}}{\rho_k(x)} - \frac{\mu_k^v}{\rho_k(x)} = g. \end{cases} \quad (21)$$

In a similar way, the minimization problem (16), (17) can be solved. Indeed, there have

$$\begin{cases} q^{v+1} = \text{shrink}\left(\nabla u^{v+1} + \frac{\mu_q^v}{\rho_q(x)}, \frac{\rho_q(x)}{\alpha(x)}\right) \\ \frac{\mu_q^{v+1}}{\rho_q(x)} - \frac{\mu_q^v}{\rho_q(x)} = \nabla u^{v+1} - q^{v+1} \end{cases}, \quad (22)$$

and

$$\begin{cases} h^{v+1} = \text{shrink}\left(\nabla^2 u^{v+1} + \frac{\mu_h^v}{\rho_h(x)}, \frac{\rho_h(x)}{\tau(x)}\right) \\ \frac{\mu_h^{v+1}}{\rho_h(x)} - \frac{\mu_h^v}{\rho_h(x)} = \nabla^2 u^{v+1} - h^{v+1} \end{cases}, \quad (23)$$

In summary, an alternating minimization algorithm of the MLG-TVBH model is given as follows.

Algorithm Given a tolerance $\epsilon_0 > 0$. Choose initial guess $u^0, k^0 = \mu_k = 0, q^0 = \mu_q = 0, h^0 = \mu_h = 0, \theta^0$.

Set $v = 0$, do

Step 1. Calculate φ^{v+1} by equation (9).

Step 2. Calculate u^{v+1} by (19),(20).

Step 3. Calculate $k^{v+1}, q^{v+1}, h^{v+1}$ and $\mu_k^{v+1}, \mu_q^{v+1}, \mu_h^{v+1}$ by (21)-(23), respectively.

If $|u^{v+1} - u|/|u^v| \leq \epsilon_0$, end the recurrence. Otherwise, go to the next steps.

Step 4. Calculate θ^{v+1} by (12), (13).

Step 5. Set v=v+1, go to step 1.

It can be seen that only step 2 is time-consuming, while the others can be calculated explicitly.

III. APPLICATIONS

In this section, the proposed method is applied for image denoising with H representing the identity operator and data reconstruction with H representing the Abel transform [15] [16], i.e.,

$$Hu(x,y) = 2\int_{|x|}^{T} \frac{ru(r,y)}{\sqrt{r^2 - x^2}} dr. \quad (24)$$

The intensity of the observed image is rescaled to the interval [0,1] before operation. Some synthetic images are utilized, and degenerated versions are obtained by adding random noise to the clean ones with certain proportion. The programs were coded in C++ and run on a personal computer with four 2.83 GHz CPU processors.

A. *Configuration of* ρ

Based on the ideas in [9][16], the second-order total variation is used to restrain the staircase effect in the restored images. Meanwhile, the strictly positive penalty functions ρ_q, ρ_h, and ρ_k act as stopping functions preventing from over-blurring. The stopping functions can be defined by

$$\rho_q = 1\Big/\sqrt{1 + \left(|\nabla G_{\sigma_0} * u|/K_q\right)^2},$$
$$\rho_h = 1\Big/\left(\sqrt{1 + \left(|\nabla G_{\sigma_0} * u|/K_h\right)^2}\right)^3,$$

and

$$\rho_k(x) = \exp(-\rho_q(x)),$$

respectively, where G_{σ_0} is the Gaussian filter with fixed parameter σ_0, '$*$' denote the convolution operator. In application, K_q, K_h are positive valve with $K_q \gg K_h$. The former is the valve of true edges in the original image, and the other is used to distinguish pseudo signal caused by the staircase effect.

B. *The numerical scheme for (19)*

It is noted that there have been many approaches of computing u in the literature, such as steepest descent method (e.g., [17]), lagged-diffusivity fixed-point method (e.g., [18]), additive operator splitting (AOS, e.g., [19], [20]), dual method (e.g., [21]), and so on.

In this paper, the gradient descent method and the semi-implicit AOS scheme are utilized to get the solution of (19). Intuitively, in homogeneous regions of a given image, $|\nabla^2 u|$ is significantly smaller than $|\nabla u|$, and thus, integrate the fourth-order divergence term into the source term W, and consider the following evolution equation

$$u_t - \mathrm{div}(\rho_q \nabla u) = -\mathrm{div}^2(\rho_h \nabla^2 u) - W(u, f) \qquad (25)$$

with initial-boundary conditions. It can be seen that the stopping functions ρ_q, ρ_h are fundamental in our method, since isotropic diffusion is undesired as they are spatially invariable.

To meet the boundary condition, we utilize the trick of continuous extension to the boundary of original images. The scale derivative term, i.e., u_t, is approximated by a forward difference scheme. The first-order divergence term is approx -imated by the standard central difference, and the second-order divergence term is approximated by finite forward and/or backward differences (e.g., [9]). Hence, equation (25) can be solved by a semi-implicit AOS scheme, which can be used to deal with the heat flow equation to compute the Gaussian convolution.

Additionally, to assess the reconstruction performance, the quality index of restoration

$$\mathrm{PSNR} = 10\lg\left(255^2 / \frac{1}{F_h F_v}\sum_{i,j=1}^{F_h F_v}(u_{i,j} - f_{i,j})^2\right) \qquad (26)$$

is adopted in this paper.

C. *Initial value and parameter selection*

In applications, we pay more attention is the selection of parameters $(\sigma_i^2)^0, i = 1,2$ and the valve value K_q than the other parameters, such as K_h, α, τ and the scale step size $(\equiv 0.1)$, since they are less sensitve and almost consistent in our experiments. For example, in this paper, $\alpha = 2, \tau = 0.1$, and $K_h = 10^{-4}$. The stopping criterion in our experiments is $\epsilon_0 = 10^{-4}$. In this paper, $\gamma_1^0 = \gamma_2^0 = 0.5$, $(\sigma_1^2)^0 = 0.5$, $(\sigma_2^2)^0 = 0.1\sim0.05$.

D. *Image denoising*

In this section, some experiments of the proposed model are listed for reconstructing images corrupted by different kinds of mixed noise.

Figure 1 shows an experiment of removing mixed Lapla ce-Gaussian noise. Figure 1A) is a synthesized image according to [10], Figure 1B) is a degenerated version of Figure 1A) with PSNR =26.45dB by adding 30% Laplace noise ($\sigma_1^2 = 0.05$) and Gaussian noise ($\sigma_2^2 = 0.05$) to Figure 1A). Figure 1C) is a recovered image using our proposed model, PSNR=33.07dB, $K_q = 0.03$.

Figure 2 presents another experiment. Figure 2A) is a synthesized image composed of two triangles and one circle. Figure 2B) is obtained by adding Laplace-Laplacian noise to Figure 2A) with PSNR=19.61dB. Figure 2C) is recovered by the proposed model with PSNR=36.25dB, $K_q = 0.045$.

Figure 3 shows the validation of mixed Gaussian noise removal. Figure 3A) is the standard Lenna image. Figure 3B) is a noisy image of Figure 3A) by additive Gaussian noise with PSNR=19.29 dB. Figure 3C) is obtained by our proposed method with PSNR =10.18dB.

E. *Object reconstruction*

In this section, we give only one experiment on the France Test Object (FTO).

In Figure 4, Figure 4A) is the original image of its density distribution. Figure 4B) is its projection image, which is corrupted by mixed Laplace ($\sigma_1^2 = 0.03, 30\%$) and Gauss ($\sigma_2^2 = 0.005$) noise. Figure 4C) is a reconstructed image of Figure 4B) using the Abel inversion formula (e.g., [15]). Figure 4D) is a reconstructed version obtained by our proposed method with parameters $\alpha = 1.5$, $\tau = 0.2$, $K_q = 0.015, K_h = 0.0002$.

IV. CONCLUSIONS AND REMARKS

In this paper, a new modeling framework is proposed, which is based on the assumption of mixed Laplace-Gaussian noise. The proposed model can be seen as an improvement of some known works, such as those in [8]-[10].

The algorithm of the proposed model is also investigated via the splitting tactics and the ALM with some modification. Spatially adaptive functions are introduced to enhance significant information in the original images. Also, a new soft shrinking formula is obtained. Numerical experiments illuminate its validation of recovering images in the presence of varies kinds of mixed noise.

The proposed model can be further extended to process images degenerated by blur and inhomogeneous light field, which is to be discussed in future work.

REFERENCES

[1] B. Zhang, M. J. Fadili, J. I. Starck, "Multiscale variance-stabilizing transform for mixed-Poission-Gaussian processes and its application in bioimaing," IEEE Interational Conference on Image Processing, 2007, pp. 233-236.

[2] A. Foi, M. Trimeche, K. Eqiazarian, "Practical Poissonian-Gaussian noise modeling and fitting for single-image raw-data,"IEEE Trans. Image Processing, 2008, vol. 17, pp. 1737-1754.

[3] J. F. Cai, R. Chan, M. Nikolova, "Two-phase methods for deblurring images corrupted by impulse plus gaussian noise, " Inverse Problem Imaging, 2008, vol. 2, pp. 187-204.

[4] J. Liu, X.-C. Tai, H.-Y. Huang, Z.-D. Huan, "A weighted dictionary learning model for denoising images corrupted by mixed noise," IEEE Trans. Image Processing, 2013, vol. 22(3), pp. 1108-1120.

[5] J. Delon, A. Desolneux A, "A patch-based Approach for removing impulse or mixed Gaussian-impulse noise," SIAM J. Imaging Sciences, 2013, vol. 6(2), pp. 1140-1174.

[6] J. Liu, H.-Y. Huang, Z.-D. Huan, H.-L. Zhang, "Adaptive variational method for restoring color images with high

density impulse noise," Inter. J. Comput. Vis., 2010, vol. 90, pp. 131-149.

[7] M. Hintermüller, A. Langer,. "Subspace correction methods for a class fo nonsmooth and nonadditive convex variational problems with mixed L^1/L^2 data fidelity in image processing," SIAM J. Imaging Sci., 2013, vol. 6(4), pp. 2134-2173.

[8] Z.Gong, Z. Shen, K. C. Toh, "Image restoration with mixed or unknown," Multiscale Model. Simul., 2014, vol.12(2), pp. 458-487.

[9] F. Li, C.-M. Shen, J. Fan, C.-L. Shen, "Image restoration combining a total variational filter and a fourth-order filter," J. Vis. Commun. Image R., 2007, vol. 18, pp. 322-330.

[10] K. Papafitsoros, C.B. Shcönlieb, "A combined First and second order variational approach for image reconstruction," J. Math. Imaging Vis., 2014, vol. 48, pp. 308-338.

[11] J. Idier,. Bayesian approach to inverse problems. Wiley, New York, 2008.

[12] J.Liu, H.-L. Zhang, "Image segmentation using a local GMM in a variational framework," J. Math. Imaging Vis., 2013, vol.46, pp. 161-176.

[13] D. P. Bertsekas, J. N. Tsitsiklis, "Parallel and distributed computation: numerical methods," Athena Scientific, Belmont, Massachusetts, 1997.

[14] V. P. Gopi, P. Palanisamy P, K. A. Wahid, "Micro-CT image reconstruction based on alternating direction augmented Lagrangian method and total variation," Comput. Medical Imaging Graph., 2013, vol. 37, pp. 419-429.

[15] R. Abraham, M. Bergounioux, E. Trélat, "A penalization approach for tomographic reconstruction of binary axially symmetric objects," Appl. Math. Optim., 2008, vol.58, pp. 345-371.

[16] R. H. Chan, H. Liang, S. Wei, M. Nikolova, X.C. Tai, "High-order total variation regularization approach for axially symmetric object tomography from a single radiograph," Inverse Problems & Imaging, 2015, Vol.9(1), pp. 55-77.

[17] A. Chambolle, P. L. Lions,"Image recovery via total variation minimization and related problems," Numer. Math., 1997, vol.76, pp. 167-188.

[18] M. Lysaker, X.-C. Tai, "Iterative image restoration combining total variation minimization and a second-order functional," Int. J. Comput. Vis., 2006, vol.66(1), pp. 5-18.

[19] T.-T. Wu, Y.-F. Yang, Z.-F. Pang, " A modified fixed-point iterative algorithm for image restoration using fourth-order PDE model, " Applied Numer. Math., 2012, vol. 62, pp. 79-90.

[20] T. Lu, P. Neittaanmaki, and X.-C. Tai, "A parallel splitting up method and its application to Navier-Stokes equations," Applied Mathematics Letters, 1991, vol.4(2), pp. 25-29.

[21] J. Weickert, B. ter Haar Romeny, and M. Viergever, "Efficient and reliable schemes for nonlinear diffusion filtering," IEEE Trans. Image Proc., 1998, vol.7, pp. 398-410.

[22] A.Chambolle, T. Pock, "A first-order primal-dual algorithm for convex problems with applications to imaging," J. Math. Imaging Vis., 2011, vol.40(1), pp. 120-145.

Figure 1. A) (Left) An synthesized noise-free image[10]; B) (Center) Mixed Gaussian-Laplacian noise added to A); C) (Right) Restored version by our model.

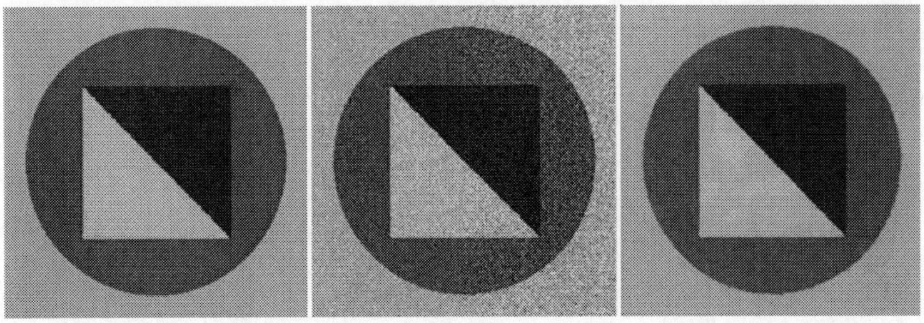

Figure 2. A) (Left) A synthesized image; B) (Center) Mixed Laplacian-Laplacian noise ;C) (Right) A restored version using our proposed model.

Figure 3. A) (Left) Lenna image; B) (Center) A noisy version of A) by adding mxied Gaussian noise; C) (Right) A restored version obtianed by our proposed method

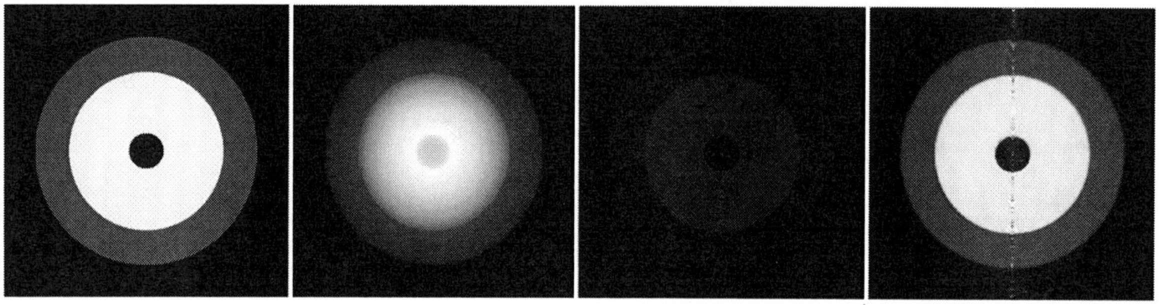

Figure 4. A) (Left) The original density distribution image of FTO; B) (MidLeft) A degenerated image of the projection of A), obtianed by utilizing the Abel formulation (20) firstly, and then adding mixed Laplace-Gauss noise. C) (MidRight) A reconstructed image of B) using the Abel Inverse formula [15] D) (Right) A reconstructed image using our proposed method.

Search Opportunities of Swarming Particles Methods in Irregular Multi-Extreme Enviroments

Rudolf Neydorf, Ivan Chernogorov
Department of Software Computer Technology and Automated Systems
Don State Technical University
Rostov-on-Don, Russia
Email: ran_pro@mail.ru, hintaivr@gmail.com

Dean Vucinic
Vesalius College
Vrije Universiteit Brussel (VUB)
Faculty of Electrical Engineering, Computer Science and Information Technology (FERIT)
Josip Juraj Strossmayer University of Osijek
Email: dean.vucinic@vub.ac.be, dean.vucinic@ferit.hr

Abstract— **The paper studies the actual task of developing and setting up the algorithms for multi-extreme objects search optimization. To solve such problems, the heuristic methods are effectively used, in particular applying the swarming particles method. The mathematical base for the modified swarming particles method, which is oriented to solve the multi-extreme search problems, is developed and described in detail. The modified algorithm is applied to the irregular multi-extreme Lambda test functions, considered to be a very difficult test case. The developed "Lambda Function" software is created to control the generation, editing and investigation of multidimensional multi-extreme test functions. The applied Lambda function is a multiplicative function developed by R. Neydorf, with fundamental extremes, multidimensionality and isolation in the factor space, which completely exclude the influence of the computed results. The application of this fundamentally new test function shows that such modified method of swarming particles is suitable for solving rather complex multi-extreme search problems. In addition, the developed "Lambda Function" software shows wide range of application possibilities when developing and researching the test functions for other related applications.**

Keywords-search optimization; multi-extreme; method of swarming particles; test functions; irregularity; software.

I. INTRODUCTION

Many modern technical and scientific problems are complex, as they need to solve optimization problems [1]. Today, most of the known search engine optimization methods are designed and used to find one optimum, which is often the global one. However, the goal is not always to find only the global optimal solution. In many cases, there are many suboptimal and close to the global optimal extreme solutions, which are quite acceptable. To study such problems and find solutions applying the Multi-Extreme (ME) optimization, subject-oriented methods, as well as tools for testing and evaluation, are required.

When making decisions regarding ME, it is necessary to take into account that the deterministic search methods are usually very sensitive to their essential nonlinear continuum dependencies (in particular to discontinuity of their derivatives and variables). When searching the discrete quotient spaces, ME problems are often NP-complete [1]. In this regard, to solve complex (multidimensional and ME) optimization problems, more and more often various effective heuristic methods are applied.

The most important advantages of the heuristic algorithms, over other types of optimization algorithms, are in analogies that generated them. They consider the adaptation processes found in living and inanimate nature. Methodologically, they are based on processes found in the knowledge areas as decision-making theory, fuzzy logic, neural networks, evolutionary-genetic mechanisms, fleece behavior, etc. These processes partially repeat and in many ways supplement each other [2][3]. The disadvantages of these methods are that they are not adaptable to support analytical research and evaluation.

Today, the heuristic methods are used to solve problems of high computational complexity. One of the most promising representatives of such methods is the Method of Swarming Particles (MSP) [2]. However, the peculiarity of research and practical development of ME optimization algorithms are coming with their own complexity, cumbersomeness and significant development times, when a large number of extremes in the factor space of the related problem has to be solved.

The impossibility in performing theoretical studies of qualitative properties and numerical settings of heuristic algorithms implies that their performance and efficiency are most often checked with so-called Test functions (TFs) [4]-[6]. When algorithms for investigating ME objects are in development, the selection of effective testing tools is the problem. It is well known that TFs have either one global extreme, or they have a regular character with respect to the extremes location, and the magnitude of their respective amplitudes [7]-[10]. Thus, to have a more effective testing, the irregular multidimensional ME functions need to be created.

The most famous and widely used ME optimization TFs are: Rosenbrock [7], Rastrigin [8], Himmelblau [9], De Jong [7], Griewank [7], Schwefel [7], etc. In addition, many papers describe other variants of TFs that generates ME functions [10]. They ensure a good verification of the ME optimization algorithms, the quality of the structural and parametric setup has to be controlled to study the factor space. In this context, a structural evaluation means the determination of the number of extremes and their spatial arrangement (coordinates). The parametric estimation means the determination of the extremes magnitudes (taking into account their signs).

The disadvantage of most TFs is their regular and analytical character. The absence of no differentiable or poorly differentiable areas greatly facilitates the work on the algorithm, by evaluating the surface shape under investigation. The real search is made difficult due to the fact that their coordinates are usually close to each other. The presence of noticeable surface curvature at the respective extreme distance facilitates its search. Therefore, the TF extreme should be as close as possible to the impulse form, as in such case its neighborhood is minimally curved. A sufficiently developed adaptive algorithm can easily identify the period of the extremes alternation.

In Section 2, the problem described in this paper is formulated. Section 3 contains a description of the Multiplicatively Allocating Function (MAF) and its characteristics. Section 4 illustrates the features of the developed special software (SW) for MAF building. Section 5 describes the mathematical model (MM) of modified MSP for ME search. Section 6 shows the result of experiments on the generated Lambda TFs. Section 7 contains the conclusion of the conducted research and future work.

II. PROBLEM FORMULATION

Following the above described issues, the goal of this paper is to develop and study the MSP modification, aiming to solve different ME search problems. For testing and setting a highly efficient solution to treat these problems, it is necessary to test the MSP on TFs, which are coming with disadvantages, as already described in the introduction. Thus, it is necessary to implement algorithmically and programmatically the TF generator, which is theoretically presented in [4], and to conduct and process statistically the representative experiments, when setting up the modified MSP.

III. SCALABLE MAF FOR EXTREME FORMING

R. Neydorf et al. developed the general principles for constructing the universal irregular ME TFs, based on the application of MAF suitable constructed to approximate problems [4]-[6].

MM of such MAF for N-dimensional ME TF, with a number of K extremes, has the form:

$$\lambda(\vec{x}) = \sum_{k=1}^{K}[a_k \prod_{i=1}^{N} \lambda_{x_i k}(x_i, x_{ik}, \Delta x_{ik}, e_{ik})] \qquad (1)$$

where: x *vector* – is an N-dimensional values vector, x *vector* $\in \{x_1, x_2, x_3, \ldots, x_n\}$; a_k – is a coefficient specifying the extreme value.

Figure 1 demonstrates the modeling of 3 λ-functions maxima in 2-dimensional space having different pulse fronts edge steepness (2). Variant A is impulse extreme (e_{ik}=0.1), B is intermediate variant (e_{ik}=0.5), C is shelving extreme (e_{ik}=1).

$$\begin{aligned} &\lambda_{x_i k}(x_i, x_{ik}, \Delta x_{ik}, e_{ik}) = \\ &= [x_i - x_{idk} + \sqrt{(x_i - x_{idk})^2 + e_{ik}^2}\,]* \\ &*[x_{iuk} - x_i + \sqrt{(x_{iuk} - x_i)^2 + e_{ik}^2}\,]/ \\ &/(4\sqrt{[(x_i - x_{idk})^2 + e_{ik}^2]\cdot[(x_{iuk} - x_i)^2 + e_{ik}^2]}) \end{aligned} \qquad (2)$$

where: $\{x_{ik}, \Delta x_{ik}, e_{ik}\}$ – is the set of TF parameters; $x_{idk} = x_{ik} - \Delta x_{ik}$, $x_{iuk} = x_{ik} + \Delta x_{ik}$ – are the initial and final coordinates of extreme pulse for x *vector*; e_{ik} – is the edge steepness parameter.

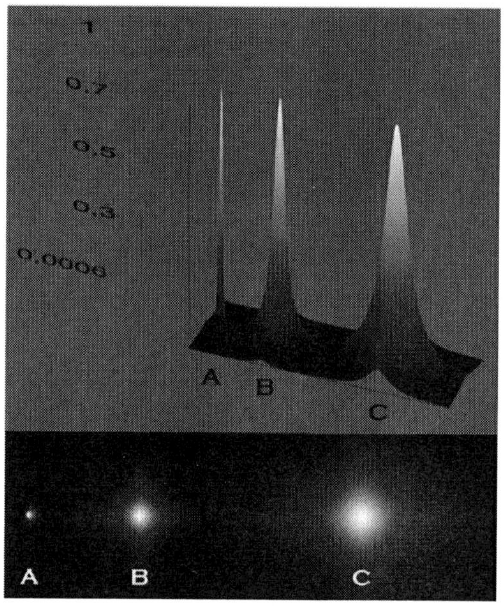

Figure 1. Different pulse fronts steepness of λ-function extrema

The graphs are constructed from (1) and (2).

IV. SOFTWARE IMPLEMENTATION OF Λ-GENERATOR

The SW for TFs creation is developed with C# programming language. It is a MAF research tool. The SW is a desktop application with third-party library for visualization, which is a part of the executable file to simplify its execution.

The "Lambda Function" features are:

- Russian and English interface languages;
- Create / load / save / delete the test. The test is saved in the XML format. This feature allows user to use the resulting TF to effectively check the optimization algorithm within the third-party program without the use of additional technologies;
- Multidimensionality;
- Adding (editing) extremes in 2 modes: 1st - manual input and 2nd - pseudo-random generation of parameter values in the specified ranges;
- Display and save the resulting TF equation in analytical form;

- Validation of all input data;
- Visualization of the TF graph with the cut-off points to display multidimensional TF and 2-display modes for 2D and 3D graphs.

Figures 2 and 3 illustrate the SW capabilities (2D and 3D models). Figure 2 shows a user function with 50 maxima (equal in magnitude of amplitudes, increments and steepness of pulse fronts). Figure 3 demonstrates a generated function with 31 maxima (different amplitudes, increments and steepness of the pulse fronts).

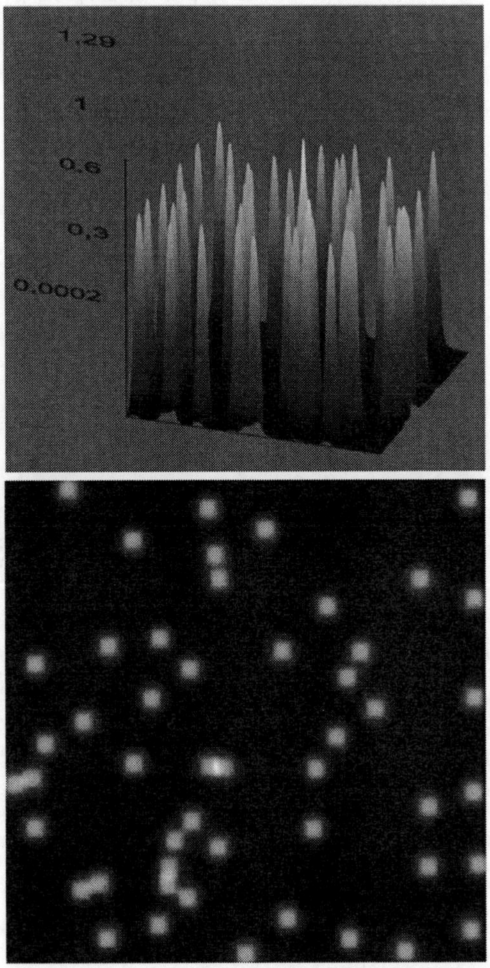

Figure 2. Demonstration of different steepness of pulse fronts of λ-function extrema

V. MSP MM, MODIFIED FOR ME SEARCH

The essence for using MSP in search optimization problems is well known [1][2]. The classical MSP algorithm imitates the real group behavioral insects, birds, fish, many protozoa, etc. However, the ME optimization requires some specific algorithm properties. Therefore, the canonical MSP version has been significantly revised and modified by the authors [2][3]. The hybrid algorithm includes basic algorithm laws of mechanics, dynamics, gravitation and stochastic "blurring" of the method parameters, which are used in the swarm prototype. In particular, its modification has been developed for solving ME problems in multidimensional spaces.

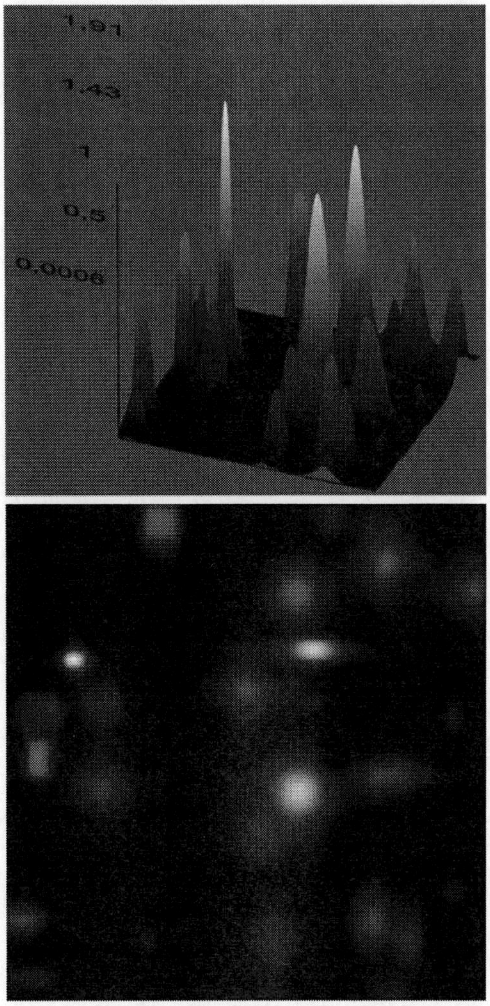

Figure 3. Example of generated ME TF with impulses of different steepness

MSP MM is constructed from the basic kinematic motion equations of the material point for the particle position and velocity:

$$\vec{X}_{ti} = \vec{X}_{(t-\Delta t)i} + \vec{V}_{(t-\Delta t)i} \cdot \Delta t \quad (3)$$

$$\vec{V}_{ti} = \vec{V}_{(t-\Delta t)i} + \vec{A}_{(t-\Delta t)i} \cdot \Delta t \quad (4)$$

where: $\vec{X}_{(t-\Delta t)i}$ - is previous particle position; $\vec{V}_{(t-\Delta t)i}$ - is previous particle velocity; Δt - is time interval (iteration); $\vec{A}_{(t-\Delta t)i}$ - is particle acceleration at previous iteration, where:

$$\vec{A}_i = \sum \frac{\hat{D}_i^Q g^Q m_i^Q}{(r_i^Q)^2 + (\varepsilon^Q)^2} - \\ - \mu_{vis} \vec{V}_{(t-\Delta t)i} - \mu_{tur} \left| \vec{V}_{(t-\Delta t)i} \right| \vec{V}_{(t-\Delta t)i} \quad (5)$$

where: $\sum \frac{\hat{D}_i^Q g^Q m_i^Q}{(r_i^Q)^2 + (\varepsilon^Q)^2}$ - is the acceleration caused by the bio-analog of particles gravitational attraction to the extreme point, $Q \in \{G, L_i\}$, G - is the particle attraction to the global swarm extreme; L_i - the best found position by particle for all time; $\hat{D}_i^Q$ - is the unit director vector towards the point of attraction; g^Q - is the gravitational constant prototype; m_i^Q - is the gravity center mass; r_i^Q - is the distance between particle position and diffuse position of the attraction target point; ε^Q - is a natural acceleration limiter that excludes the passage of any material point at $\Delta X < \varepsilon$ distance; $-\mu_{vis}\vec{V}_{(t-\Delta t)i}$ - is the viscosity friction; $-\mu_{tur}\left|\vec{V}_{(t-\Delta t)i}\right|\vec{V}_{(t-\Delta t)i}$ - is the turbulent friction; μ_{vis}, μ_{tur}- are the coefficients of viscosity and turbulent friction, respectively.

To take into account the MM stochastic behavioral components, the equation of parameters random fluctuation (distortion) is included:

$$\lambda^{\xi}(\varphi) = \lambda \cdot (1 + 2\varphi \cdot (rnd(1) - 0.5)) \quad (6)$$

where: λ - is the nominal value of fluctuating parameter; φ - is the coefficient of parameter distortion, relative to the nominal value; $rnd(1)$ - is the random float number in [0;1] range. This law applies to the following collective parameters of a swarm and particles:

- Prototypes of gravitational constants - g^Q;
- Coefficients of viscosity and turbulent friction - μ_{vis} and μ_{tur};
- Dissipation coefficient - μ_{dis}.

VI. MSP MODIFICATION FOR A TFS APPLICATION

To study and adjust the ME modification of MSP, 3 demonstration Lambda TFs are generated using the "Lambda Function" SW; see Figures 4(a), 4(b) and 4(c). In addition, to test the MSP modification, an appropriate "MMSP" (Modified MSP) SW was developed. For its development, the C # programming language was used.

For all experiments, the same particle number (P) and iteration (I) settings were used, to obtain a more general picture of MSP operation on various generated functions. At the same time, the dynamics parameters were settings dynamically, with respect to the region under consideration.

Figures 4(d), 4(e) and 4(f) show Lambda functions and localized MSP regions (red squares) and extremes (blue dots), which are found and evaluated. Each function has a specific feature that allows you to identify the positive aspects and disadvantages of the optimization algorithm being developed.

Figures 4(a) and 4(d) show a TF with 5 minima and 3 maxima. The functions are steep near extremes and moderately canopies at the bases, and being located at a considerable distance from each other. However, the amplitude of the extremes is not high (-1), and it is not easy to identify the whole set of extremes from the first pass.

Figures 4(b) and 4(e) illustrate the generated function with 20 maxima. This function is complicated by the fact that the extremes have steep pulses. Outside the extremes region, agents have virtually no information about remote impulses. Only the mechanism of interaction between particles in the swarm, as part of the MSP MM modification, has enabled to investigate this type of function.

Figures 4(c) and 4(f) show a Lambda function, which has 8 minima and 8 maxima to identify and estimate the minima. The shape of this function is similar to the bends of "peaks" and "gorges," which can be smooth, but may have sharp cliffs. By localizing one of the extremes, the multi-agent system is not exploring the rest of the search space. However, this does not happen in the modified MSP.

Tables I-III show the experiments results of a successful search for the modified-MSP. These results were obtained from the basic MM motion of the swarm (preceding the MM clustering mechanism [11], which divided the search space into subspaces and found in each an extreme, and which was replaced by the dynamic clustering caused by the behavioral model of the swarm itself). The agents localize extreme areas, under the influence of attraction forces (not only global, but also local). The increase in the influence of local attraction is caused, in particular, by the introduction of a turbulent deceleration in the MM. The removal of the non-dynamic clustering mechanism from MM also enabled to exclude the "cluster" attraction of the swarm particles to the closest previously created clusters, which allowed the particles to behave in a more similar way to the real prototype.

As a result, the minimum error of the obtained approximation in experiment 1 (see Table I), relative to the standard, was ~0.01%, average ~0.03%. MSP successfully isolated the extreme regions and obtained the described results due to the smooth motion of the particles to the extreme values found at the moment (based on (3)-(5)). This allowed the particles not to jump through the extremes.

The minimum error of the obtained approximation in experiment 2 (see Table II), relative to the standard, turned out to be ~0.001%, mean ~0.01%. The parameter of the slope of the pulse fronts of a given Lambda function for all extremes is 0.01, which implies the complexity in finding them. However, since the number of extremes is 20, the particles interact with each other and receive an additional opportunity to study the neighboring extremes. This effect is due to the fact that, when the particle is found close to a extreme, then, in the next step, it will get a large acceleration (see (5)), which will allow the particle to escape from this extreme attraction zone and visit the extreme region of the neighboring one.

The minimum error of the approximation obtained in experiment 3 (see Table III), relative to the standard, was ~0.09%, average ~3%.

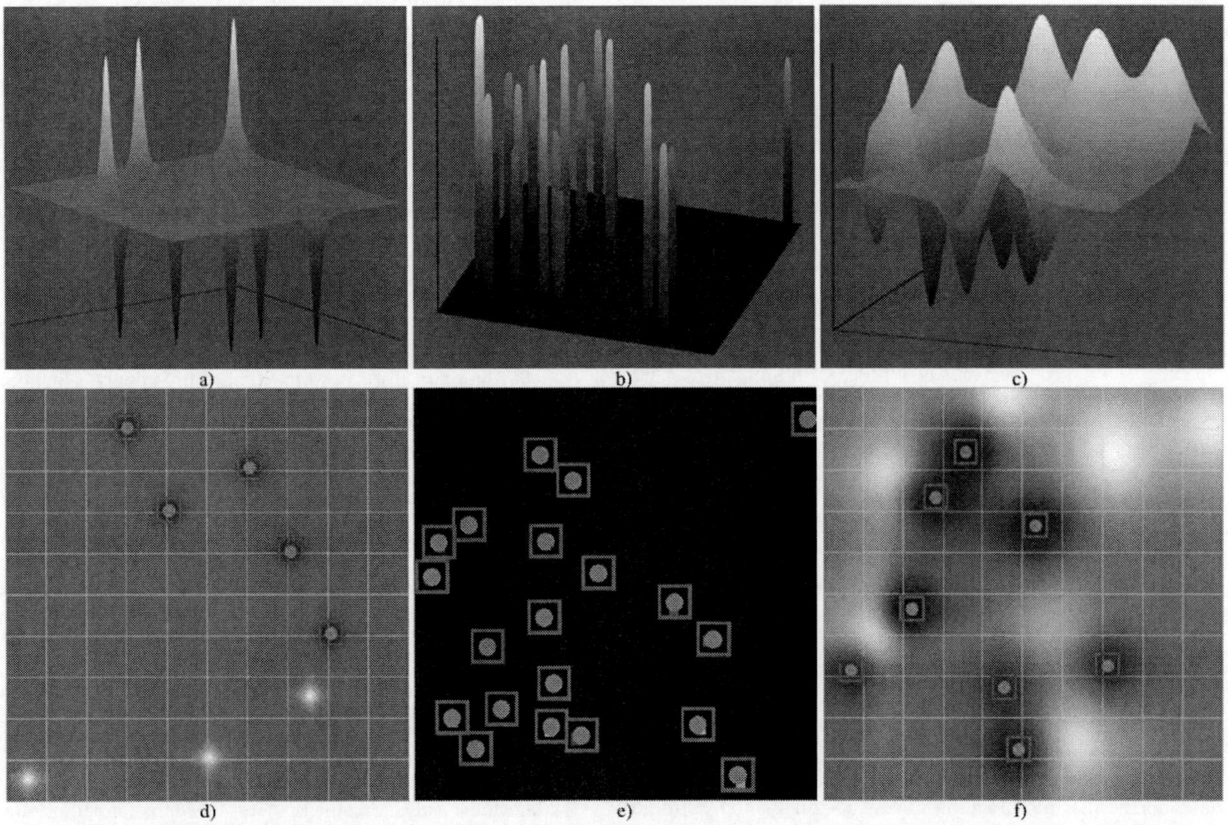

Figure 4. Generated TF graphs and MSP result on different scenes: *a* – I on 3D, *b* – II on 3D, *c* – III on 3D, *d* – I on 2D, *e* – II on 2D, *f* – III on 2D

TABLE I. I A TF STANDARD AND MSP RESULT

Standard			MSP		
x	*y*	*f(x, y)*	*x*	*y*	*f(x, y)*
70.5	60.5	-1	70.4811	60.4904	-0.9998
30.5	90.5	-1	30.5206	90.5171	-0.9998
60.5	80.5	-1	60.4901	80.5104	-0.9999
80.5	40.5	-1	80.5486	40.5173	-0.9993
40.5	70.5	-1	40.5158	70.4641	-0.9996

The complexity of this experiment consists in mixing maxima and minima. This means that the particles will be located more often in positions that may be worse than their previous ones. However, the method is also effective in such a case.

TABLE II. II A TF STANDARD AND MSP RESULT

Standard			MSP		
x	*y*	*f(x, y)*	*x*	*y*	*f(x, y)*
6.4254	4.6182	0.4543	6.4253	4.6182	0.4543
3.2322	4.4678	0.7859	3.2322	4.4698	0.7859
9.7602	9.2187	0.6206	9.7505	9.2172	0.6206
1.3463	6.6313	0.5903	1.3412	6.6291	0.5903
3.9888	1.4936	0.4183	3.99	1.4981	0.4183
…					
4.5307	5.4641	0.7796	4.5327	5.4604	0.7796
2.1397	2.2475	0.5101	2.1423	2.2536	0.5101
3.3574	1.6594	0.8659	3.3518	1.6565	0.8659
0.9593	1.9634	0.9677	0.9597	1.9561	0.9677
1.4741	1.2706	0.7321	1.473	1.2718	0.7321
7.2637	3.8593	0.5123	7.2631	3.8621	0.5123

TABLE III. III A TF STANDARD AND MSP RESULT

Standard			MSP		
x	*y*	*f*(*x*, *y*)	*x*	*y*	*f*(*x*, *y*)
3.6721	8.491	-0.5598	3.6181	8.451	-0.5651
5.3615	6.6256	-0.5653	5.343	6.6296	-0.5658
0.7982	3.1601	-0.2936	0.7953	3.1288	-0.2901
4.9938	1.1940	-0.4426	4.8912	1.1833	-0.455
4.5671	2.7411	-0.2833	4.5894	2.6884	-0.2849
2.025	4.5505	-0.5831	2.1631	4.6302	-0.6375
2.6129	7.4111	-0.4821	2.769	7.3498	-0.5187
7.0786	3.2646	-0.3418	7.1416	3.2602	-0.3451

The attraction of particles to the global extreme allows improving the result of the whole swarm, even in a situation where the best position of the particle itself is not a local extreme (which forces the particle to swarm in the pseudo-local area). With additional sub-optimization of the parameters of the swarm and particles, the error can be significantly reduced [2][3].

VII. Conclusion and Future Work

The developed Lambda Function SW has proven to be an effective tool for the generation of the irregular multi-dimensional ME TFs. The easy-to use and convenient interface to access the multi-functional SW allows the fast generation and qualitative analysis of TFs. The demonstrated SW functions do not have an obvious regular and analytical character, like the set of the today existing ME optimization TFs.

The experiments carried out on TFs showed that the developed MSP modification allows localizing the extreme areas of the nonstandard irregular ME Lambda function, having the approximation error from ~0.001% to ~3%.

The experimentally obtained results allow the validation of the developed MSP modification, and prove that the developed Lambda Function SW is an effective tool in searching the extremes of heterogeneous generated TFs.

The main research outcome is the modified heuristic method of swarming particles applied to the author's Cut-Glue approximation for highly nonlinear dependencies.

The developed generator, in addition to the presented advantages has the possibility of creating irregular multidimensional ME TFs with MAF modification. Thus, it further helps to investigate the properties of TFs, when they are applied to different domains, and allowing more accurate results analysis of the overall "Cut-Glue" approximations approach.

References

[1] R. Shreves, Drupal search engine optimization, Birmingham: Packt Publishing LTD, 2012.

[2] R. Neydorf et al., "Study of Search Optimization Opportunities of Heuristic Algorithms for Solving Multi-Extremal Problems," Proceedings of The X International Conference on Advanced Engineering Computing and Applications in Sciences ADVCOMP2016, IARIA XPS Press, Venice, Italy, 2016. pp. 44-51.

[3] R. Neydorf et al., "Formal Characterization and Optimization of Algorithm for the Modelling of Strongly Nonlinear Dependencies Using the Method "Cut-Glue" Approximation of Experimental Data," SAE Technical Paper, doi:10.4271/2016-01-2033, 2016.

[4] R Neydorf, "Advanced test function for studying the multi-extremal problems and solutions," Proceedings of the VI International Seminar "System analysis, Management and Information processing", Rostov-on-Don, Russia, 2015, pp. 6-14.

[5] R. Neydorf, "Bivariate "Cut-Glue" Approximation of Strongly Nonlinear Mathematical Models Based on Experimental Data," SAE Int. J. Aerosp. 8(1), 2015, pp. 47-54.

[6] R. Neydorf and I. Chernogorov "Universal Generator of Irregular Multidimensional Multiextremal Test Functions," Proceedings of the XXX International Scientific Conference Mathematical methods in technique and technologies - MMTT-30, vol. 2, 2017, pp. 138-143.

[7] M. Molga and C. Smutnicki, "Test functions for optimization needs," Technical Report, Institute of Computer Engineering Control and Robotics, Wroclaw University of Technology, Wroclaw, Poland, 2005.

[8] L. A. Rastrigin, Systems of extremal control, Nauka Publishing House, Moscow, Russia, 1974.

[9] D. Himmelblau, Applied Nonlinear Programming, McGraw-Hill, New York, USA, 1972.

[10] M. Laguna and R. Marti, "Experimental Testing of Advanced Scatter Search Designs for Global Optimization of Multimodal Functions," Journal of Global Optimization archive, vol. 33, issue 2, 2005, pp. 235-255.

[11] Roman, "Clustering. Algorithm A-quasiequivalence," https://habrahabr.ru/post/124978 [retrieved: March 2017].

Numerical Study for Unsteady Aerodynamics of Multi-Dimensional Freely Falling Plates or Thin Coins

Changqiu Jin
Institute of Applied Physics and Computational Mathematics, Beijing, China
e-mail: jin_changqiu@iapcm.ac.cn

Abstract—**This paper presents a multi-dimensional high-order gas-kinetic scheme on moving mesh to simulate unsteady flows of freely falling plates or thin coins. The two-dimensional scheme has previously been successfully implemented on freely falling plates, where the rich dynamical behavior, such as fluttering and tumbling motion, was analyzed and the quantitative comparison has been provided between the experimental measurement and numerical computation. In the past several years, a three-dimensional gas-kinetic scheme on moving grid has also been developed to compute fluid problems with moving boundaries. In this work in progress paper, both the modified grid velocity and high-order gas-kinetic scheme are developed to improve the above gas-kinetic method, which is applied for simulating three-dimensional freely falling thin disks.**

Keywords-moving mesh method; gas-kinetic scheme; high-order scheme; freely falling plates or thin coins.

I. INTRODUCTION

It is a fact that not all falling objects travel straight downwards, such as leaves, tree seeds, and paper cards dropped from a table. Obviously, falling leaves and tumbling sheets of paper can get a lift momentarily to float upward against gravity as they flutter (oscillate from side to side) or tumble (rotate and drift sideways) through still air. To explain this complicated natural phenomenon, the knowledge of the instantaneous fluid forces is required. As we know, most objects moving in a fluid encounter unsteady aerodynamic forces. Therefore, the two-dimensional problem of falling plates has been investigated numerically by solving the Navier-Stokes equation following a moving body, where the instantaneous fluid force for the fluttering and tumbling motion has been analyzed [6].

Considering that the motion of freely falling body is usually a three-dimensional problem, further, the falling behavior of a circular thin disk has been investigated experimentally [4] [5]. Three dimensionless ratios have been proposed to characterize the flow:

$$\lambda = \frac{h}{d}, \quad I^* = \frac{\pi \rho_d}{64 \rho_f} \lambda, \quad Re = \frac{Ud}{\gamma},$$

The geometric aspect-ratio parameter λ is small for thin disks, with dimensionless moment of inertia I^* and the Reynolds number *Re,* which are most important for describing the dynamics of the disk motion. The free-fall motion of three-dimensional bodies is more complex due to an extra degree of freedom, so numerical simulation becomes more difficult as well. The gas-kinetic scheme on moving mesh for calculating two-dimensional freely falling plates [1] has been developed to simulate three-dimensional viscous fluids with moving boundaries [2]. In this work in progress paper, both the modified grid velocity distribution and high-order scheme are developed to improve the above gas-kinetic method, which has been applied for simulating three-dimensional freely falling thin disks. The complicated dynamics behavior of three-dimensional free-fall thin coins is obtained numerically.

This paper is organized as follows. Firstly, Section 2 introduces the three-dimensional high-order gas-kinetic scheme with the modified grid velocity. Secondly, Section 3 shows some formulation for the free-fall motion of a circular thin disk in still water with a focus on the planar zigzag motion. Thirdly, in Section 4, the rich fluid dynamics behavior is analyzed by subsequent numerical results which are also compared with experimental data and figures.

II. THREE-DIMENSIONAL HIGH-ORDER GAS-KINETIC SCHEME ON MOVING MESH

Under a generalized coordinate transformation with arbitrary grid velocity, the gas-kinetic Bhatnagar-Gross-Krook (BGK) [8] equation is reformulated in a moving frame of reference. Then, a conservative gas-kinetic scheme is developed for the viscous flow computation in the moving system in Eulerian space. Due to the coupling between the grid velocity and the overall solution algorithm, the Eulerian and Lagrangian methods become two limiting cases in the current method. A fully conservative formulation can be obtained, even in the Lagrangian limit, as shown in [2].

The BGK model of the approximate Boltzmann equation in three-dimensional space can be written as:

$$f_t + uf_x + vf_y + wf_z = \frac{g - f}{\tau} \qquad (1)$$

Here, f is the gas distribution function and g is the equilibrium state approached by f. Both f and g are functions of space (x, y, z), time t, particle velocity (u, v, w), and internal variable ς. The particle collision time τ is related to the viscosity and heat conduction coefficients. In this paper, we are focusing on the modified grid velocity in the cell interface numerical flux evaluation, while both the gas-kinetic scheme on moving mesh and the high-order gas-kinetic scheme are addressed in [2] and [7], respectively.

We can rewrite the mesh velocity for each point on the cell interface as:

$$U_g = U_g^{fc} + U_g^r \qquad (2)$$

in which $U_g^{fc} = (u_g^{fc}, v_g^{fc}, w_g^{fc})$ is the grid velocity at the interface barycenter. The interface flux $F - QU_g$ is written as:

$$F - QU_g = \overline{F} - QU_g^r \qquad (3)$$

On the right hand side, the first term is the mean flux with a piecewise constant mesh velocity U_g^{fc}, which is the same as the one in [2]. For the second term, it is a correction on each interface point, which reduces the difference between the real flux crossing each interface point and the mean flux $\overline{F}$.

III. MOTION DESCRIPTION FOR FREE-FALL THIN DISK

Previously, the gas-kinetic scheme on moving mesh has been applied successfully to simulate the experiment of two-dimensional falling cards [6]. Figure 1 shows a good agreement between the two-dimensional numerical result and the experimental data in [6]. The work in [4] and [5] experimentally investigates the three-dimensional free-fall motions of a circular thin disk in still water with three different trajectories, namely, zigzag, transition, and spiral,

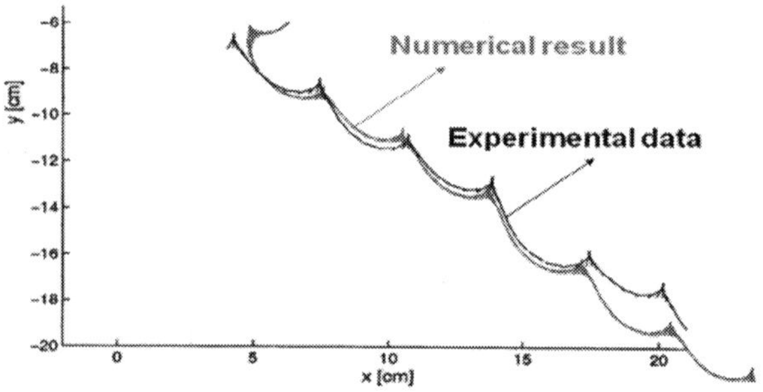

Figure 1. Computed path is compared with the experimental data .

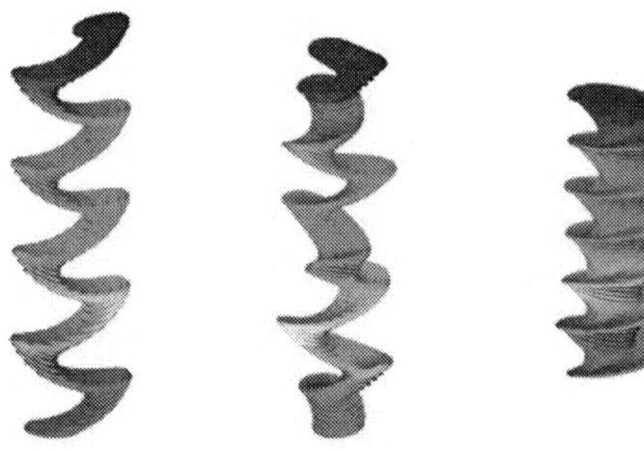

Figure 2. Free-fall motions: zigzag, transition, to spiral.

as in Figure 2. This paper focuses on the numerical simulation for the three-dimensional experiments. At present, we are working on the numerical study for the zigzag motion: namely, the description of moving trajectories and analysis for unsteady aerodynamics.

Consider the two different motions, translation and rotation. The translation acceleration is calculated by Newton law, and rotational angular acceleration is computed by the following formulas:

$$\begin{aligned} d\Omega_1/dt + (I_3 - I_2)\Omega_2\Omega_3/I_1 = 0, \\ d\Omega_2/dt + (I_1 - I_3)\Omega_1\Omega_3/I_2 = 0, \\ d\Omega_3/dt + (I_2 - I_1)\Omega_2\Omega_1/I_3 = 0, \end{aligned} \qquad (4)$$

Here, $\Omega = (\Omega_1, \Omega_2, \Omega_3)$ is angular velocity, I_1, I_2, I_3 are three principal moments of inertia.

IV. CONCLUSIONS

Based on the two-dimensional successful numerical simulation for unsteady aerodynamics of free-fall card motion [1], the three-dimensional high-order moving grid gas-kinetic scheme was developed, and was improved by the modified grid velocity and high order scheme in recent work. At present, the above method is applied to calculate the three-dimensional freely falling thin disks, and the research work of the numerical simulation is in progress. We expect to obtain a good agreement between numerical results and experimental data.

REFERENCES

[1] C. Jin and K. Xu, "Numerical study of the unsteady aerodynamics of freely falling plates", Communications in Computational Physics, vol. 3(4), pp.1815-2406, 2008.

[2] C. Jin and K. Xu, "A three-dimensional gas-kinetic scheme with moving mesh for low-speed viscous flow computation, Advances in Applied mathematics and mechanics, vol.2(6), pp.746-762,2010.

[3] S. Chen, C. Jin, and C. Lee, "Gas kinetic scheme with discontinuous derivative for low speed flow computation", Journal of Computational Physics, 230(5), pp. 2045-2059, 2011.

[4] H. Zhong, et al., "Experimental investigation of freely falling thin disks. Part 1. The flow structures and Reynolds number effects on the zigzag motion", Journal of Fluid Mechanics, vol.716, pp. 228-250, 2013.

[5] C. Lee, et al., "Experimental investigation of freely falling thin disks. Part 2. Transition of three-dimensional motion from zigzag to spiral", Journal of Fluid Mechanics, vol.732, pp.77-104, 2013.

[6] A. Andersen, U. Persavento, and Z. J. Wang, "Unsteady aerodynamics of fluttering and tumbling plates", Journal of Fluid Mechanics, vol.541, pp.65-90, 2005.

[7] L. Pan, K. Xu, Q. Li, and J. Li, "An efficient and accurate two-stage fourth-order gas-kinetic schem for the Euler and Navier-Stokes equations", Journal of Computational Physics, vol. 326, pp. 197-221, 2016.

[8] P. L. Bhatnagar, E. P. Gross, and M. Krook, "A model for collision process in gas Ⅰ: small amplitude process in charged and neutral one-component system, Phys. Rev., vol. 94, pp. 511, 1954

Learning to Play Mastermind Well Using the Anti-Mind with Feeback Algorithm

Jose Barahona da Fonseca

Department of Electrical Engineering and Computer Science
Faculty of Sciences and Technology
New University of Lisbon
2829-516 Caparica, Portugal,
Email: jbfo@fct.unl.pt

***Abstract*—In a previous work we developed the Anti-Mind algorithm. The Anti-Mind program simulated a good player of the Mastermind game, discovering the secret code defined by the human operator (a sequence of four integers in the interval [0 5]) very quickly. Then we used the algorithm of Anti-Mind to help and correct a human operator trying to discover the secret code defined by the computer resulting in the Anti-Mind with Feedback algorithm. In this paper, we revisited this work and developed another faster implementation of the Anti-Mind with Feedback algorithm which has the drawback that it does not know the set of next good guesses, it just compares each guess with the previous moves and accepts it if it is *coherent* with all the previous moves. Nevertheless, we introduced an option to generate the set of good guesses, i.e., the guesses that are *coherent* with all the previous moves. This implementation allows generalizing the Mastermind game to more than four digits and more than six colours. We begin to define rigorously what we mean by a guess *coherent* with a previous move, next we define what is a good guess and, then, we enunciate five hypotheses about the Anti-Mind algorithm namely one that guarantees that if we always play a good guess we will find the code in a finite bounded number of guesses. We propose a strategy to play Mastermind with the maximization of repetions at the beginning of the game which reduces the *cognitive overload* to play well and validate it with the Anti-Mind with Feedback algorithm. Finally we compare the Anti-Mind algorithm with the Ant-Mind with maximization of repetitions of the guesses through intensive simulations and conclude that the original Anti-Mind algorithm has a better average performance in terms of the number of guesses to break the secret code.**

Keywords–artificial intelligence; mastermind game; anti-mind algorithm; anti-mind with feedback algorithm

I. INTRODUCTION

It seems that the Mastermind game was invented by M. Meyerowitz in 1973 [1]. It is a two players game, the code maker and the code breaker, and the code breaker must find the secret code in at most 10 guesses. The secret code has four colours that may be of one of six colours. In each move the code breaker makes a guess of four colours and the code maker answers with the number of white pegs, *cpe*, the number of correct digits in wrong position, and the number of black pegs, the number of correct digits in right position, *cpc*. In this work the six colours will be represented by the integers in the interval [0 5]. Our algorithm was named Anti-Mind because it was originally created to break the code created by the human player. Then we created a variation of this algorithm where the human plays as the code breaker and the Anti-Mind algorithm is used to generate in each guess the set of good guesses, i.e., the guesses coherent with the previous moves. If the guess does not belong to the set of good moves, then, it is considered a bad move and the user is asked if he wants to see the set of good moves and, then, he must make another guess [2]. In this paper, we show how the human player can improve his skills using the Anti-Mind with Feedback algorithm. When it remains only one hypothesis that must be the secret code and the user is asked to guess the code without any more information. From the use of this algorithm resulted a simplified faster algorithm and a strategy of playing Mastermind.

Our simulations point to a worst case performance of the Anti-Mind algorithm of 9 guesses and Donald E. Knuth [3] showed through exhaustive simulations that his strategy guarantees a maximum of 5 guesses. He showed that the best first guess to guarantee this worst case performance is 1122. After the work of Knuth many proposals were published, e.g. [4]-[7], but no one beat the worst case performance of Knuths strategy of 5 guesses, nevertheless some works improved the average performance over all possible secret codes. Nevertheless, our algorithm is much faster than previous algorithms, since at each stage it selects randomly the next guess from the set of good guesses that are coherent with previous moves. In this sense, the Anti-Mind algorithm can be considered a stochastic algorithm. On the contrary Knuth's algorithm for each good guess generates the next set of good moves for each of the 15 possible combinations of *cpc* and *cpe* and chooses the good guess that *minimizes the maximum number of next good guesses* [3].

This paper is organized as follows. In Section 2, we describe how a good guess is defined based on the concept of the *coherence* of a guess with a previous *move*. In Section 3, we describe the Anti-Mind algorithm. In Section 4, we describe the Anti-Mind with Feedback algorithm. In Section 5, we show how the Anti-Mind with Feedback algorithm can be used to learn to play mastermind well, in Section 6, we present a faster version of the Anti-Mind with feedback algorithm, in Section 7, we present exhaustive simulation results of the Anti-Mind algorithm and the Anti-Mind algorithm with maximization of the number of repetitions of the guesses and in Section 8, we present the conclusions and possible vectors of evolution of our work.

II. DEFINITION OF A MASTERMIND GOOD GUESS

The main idea behind the Anti-Mind algorithm is the *coherence* between a guess and a previous *move*. In Definition 1, we define what is a *move*.

Definition 1: A *move* is the triplet (*guess*, *cpc*, *cpe*) where *cpc* and *cpe* result from the comparison between the *guess* and the secret code.

In Definition 2, we define what is the *coherence* between a *guess* and a previous *move*.

Definition 2: Consider a previous move, *move*, with *cpc* correct digits in right position and *cpe* correct digits in wrong position and a guess, *guess*. Considering that the comparison between the *guess* and the *move* resulted in *cpc_i* and *cpe_i*, then, the *guess* is coherent with *move* if (1) is true.

$$cpc = cpc\_i \text{ AND } cpe = cpe\_i \tag{1}$$

When a guess is coherent with all previous moves, then, we say that it is a *good guess*. On the contrary if the guess is not coherent with at least one previous move, then, we say that it is a *bad guess*. In this sense, we can say that *playing Mastermind well* happens when all guesses are *good guesses*.

So, we can define rigorously the set of good guesses as all combinations that are coherent with all previous moves. This is expressed by (2).

$$set\_good\_guesses = \{\forall combination : \forall move, cpc = cpc\_i \text{ AND } cpe = cpe\_i\} \tag{2}$$

Once obtained the set of good guesses, we can verify if a given guess is a good guess, testing if it belongs to the set of good guesses. Alternatively, we can compare the *guess* with all previous moves, and if it is coherent with all of them, then, it is a *good guess*.

III. The Anti-Mind Algorithm

After each guess, the Anti-Mind algorithm obtains the new set of good guesses and selects randomly one of them as the next guess. This is much less computationally expensive than Knuth's algorithm but the Anti-Mind algorithm has a greater worst performance of 8 guesses. In this sense, we can say that the Anti-Mind algorithm is a stochastic algorithm. So we can enunciate five hypotheses that we will show in a near future work that characterize the behaviour of the Anti-Mind algorithm based on emperical data like intensive simulations.

Hypothesis 1: The Anti-Mind algorithm always finds the secret code in less than 9 guesses if the codemaker did not make any error in *cpc* and *cpe* for all previous moves.

Hypothesis 2: When the Anti-Mind algorithm finds the secret code in 8 guesses, if the codemaker did not make any error in *cpc* and *cpe* for all previous moves, the eigth *good* guess is always the secret code. In appendix we show some *enough information* games with 8 guesses.

Hypothesis 3: If the codemaker makes errors in *cpc* and/or *cpe* in at least one previous move, then, the Anti-Mind algorithm always reaches a situation of an empty set of good guesses in less than 9 guesses.

Hypothesis 4: If the game reaches a situation where there is only one good guess, then, this good guess must be the secret code, if the codemaker did not make errors in the previous moves.

Hypothesis 5: Obtaining the new set of good guesses is equivalent to obtain all combinations/guesses that are coherent with all previous moves

The result of hypothesis 2 is the main idea behind our previous work of the Anti-Mind with an unlimited number of lies [8]. When it reaches the conclusion that there is at least one lie in previous moves, reaching the situation of an empty set of good guesses, then, it begins to test the hypothesis of one lie, removing one previous move from the set of previous moves and generating each time the set of good guesses. If it reaches a point where all manners of removing a previous move resulted in an empty set of good guesses, then, it begins to remove two previous moves and so on until it reaches a point where the set of good guesses has a cardinal 1. Then the removed previous moves are the moves with lies and the good guess must be the secret code [8].

Hypothesis 1 can be proved by exhaustive computer search, where for each possible secret code are generated all possible Mastermind games with good guesses and saved the number of guesses when the secret code is found. Since there are only 1296 possible Mastermind secret codes, this computer search is not prohibitive in terms of runtime.

The result of hypothesis 4 is the main idea behind the second version of the Anti-Mind with feedback algorithm where we do not have all good guesses in memory, and generate them whenever it is asked, comparing all combinations with the previous moves and printing the guesses that are coherent with all previous moves- see section 6.

IV. First Version of the Anti-Mind with Feedback Algorithm

In the Anti-Mind with feedback algorithm the human is the codebreaker and the computer the codemaker. At each move, the new set of good guesses is generated, and when the guess does not belong to this set, the user is asked to enter another guess. There is an option that allows the user to see all the good guesses. If it is reached a situation where only one good guess remains, the user is asked to enter the secret code without any more information, since hypothesis 3 guarantees that the remaining good guess must be the secret code. In Table I we present a game of this type.

In Algorithm 1, we describe the Anti-Mind algorithm in detail.

V. Using the Anti-Mind with Feedack Algorithm to Find a Good Playing Strategy

Since we think in terms of symbolic expressions, and taking into account our cognitive limitations, it is easier to begin with a guess with repetitions like 0111. Now if the answer is cpc=3, cpe=0, we can conclude that there exist three 1s in the last three positions, OR one 0 in the first position AND two 1s in two of the last three positions. This symbolical logical expression corresponds to the set of 20 good guesses presented in Table II.

But if for the same secret code, the first guess was 0123, the answer would be cpc=2, cpe=0, which means a much more

Algorithm 1 Anti-Mind with feedback algorithm

```
n_digits ⇐input('Number of Digits=')
dig_max ⇐input('Maximum Digit=')
n_good_guesses ⇐ (dig_max + 1)^n_digits
secret_code ⇐ generate_s_c(n_digits, dig_max)
set_good_guesses ⇐ gen_all_gs(n_digits, dig_max)
counter ⇐ 0
while n_good_guesses > 1 do
  counter ⇐ counter + 1
  guess ⇐ input('Guess =')
  cpc ⇐ calc_cpc(secret_code, guess)
  cpe ⇐ calc_cpe(secret_code, guess)
  if cpc == n_digits then
    display('You Found It')
    break
  end if
  flag_bel ⇐ see_if_bel(guess, set_good_guesses)
  if flag_bel then
    display_cpc_cpe(cpc,cpe)
    set_good_guesses ⇐
    calc_new_set(guess, cpc, cpe, set_good_guesses)
  else
    display('Bad Move')
    in=input('Want to See Good Guesses?')
    if in == 1 then
      display_g_g(set_good_guesses)
    end if
  end if
end while
if n_good_guesses = 1 then
  flag ⇐ 0
  while 1 − flag do
    guess=input('Secret Code=')
    flag ⇐ (guess == secret_code)
  end while
end if
```

complex symbolic expression: 0 and 1 are in right position OR 0 and 2 are in right position OR 0 and 3 are in right position OR 1 and 2 are in right position OR 1 and 3 are in right position OR 2 and 3 are in right position. This complex symbolical logical expression corresponds to a much greater set of 96 good guesses. In Table III we show these good guesses.

So in terms of *cognitive overload* it seams better to play in the beginning with repetitions.

VI. Second Version of the Anti-Mind with Feedback Algorithm

In the first version of the algorithm we first generate all combinations, and for each guess and cpc and cpe we generate a new set of good guesses, and we decide if the new guess is good, testing if the guess belongs to the set of good guesses. For a genarilized version of Mastermind with more digits and a greater maximum digit, this can take a lot of time in the first moves. So, inspired in this strategy, we created a new version of the algorithm where we only compare the guess with previous moves, and accept it if it is coherent with all previous moves. This algorithm does not have the information of the number of good guesses and it is impossibile the detection of an *enough information* situation, but it is much faster and we can play more difficult generalized Mastermind games inside Matlab environment. In Algorithm 2, we describe in detail this second version of the Anti-Mind with feedback algorithm.

TABLE I. Example of a Game with 8 Guesses

```
anti_mind_real(4,5,1, 1)
Number of Possible Good Guesses=1296
move 1=0111
cpc=0
cpe=1
Number of Possible Good Guesses=308
move 2=1222
cpc=1
cpe=0
Number of Possible Good Guesses=90
move 3=1333
cpc=1
cpe=0
Number of Possible Good Guesses=20
move 4=1444
cpc=0
cpe=1
Number of Possible Good Guesses=6
move 5=4320
cpc=2
cpe=2
Number of Possible Good Guesses=3
move 6=4302
cpc=1
cpe=3
Number of Possible Good Guesses=2
move 7=4023
cpc=1
cpe=3
*ENOUGH INFORMATION**
Secret Code=4230
*You Found It! in 8 Guesses, with 0 bad Guesses and 0 hints **
```

TABLE II. Set of Good Guesses After Guess 0111

0 0 1 1	0 1 0 1	0 1 1 0	0 1 1 2	0 1 1 3	0 1 1 4
0 1 1 5	0 1 2 1	0 1 3 1	0 1 4 1	0 1 5 1	0 2 1 1
0 3 1 1	0 4 1 1	0 5 1 1	1 1 1 1	2 1 1 1	3 1 1 1
4 1 1 1	5 1 1 1				

TABLE III. Set of Good Guesses After Guess 0123

0 0 0 3	0 0 2 0	0 0 2 2	0 0 2 4	0 0 2 5	0 0 3 3
0 0 4 3	0 0 5 3	0 1 0 0	0 1 0 1	0 1 0 4	0 1 0 5
0 1 1 0	0 1 1 1	0 1 1 4	0 1 1 5	0 1 4 0	0 1 4 1
0 1 4 4	0 1 4 5	0 1 5 0	0 1 5 1	0 1 5 4	0 1 5 5
0 2 2 0	0 2 2 2	0 2 2 4	0 2 2 5	0 3 0 3	0 3 3 3
0 3 4 3	0 3 5 3	0 4 0 3	0 4 2 0	0 4 2 2	0 4 2 4
0 4 2 5	0 4 3 3	0 4 4 3	0 4 5 3	0 5 0 3	0 5 2 0
0 5 2 2	0 5 2 4	0 5 2 5	0 5 3 3	0 5 4 3	0 5 5 3
1 1 1 3	1 1 2 1	1 1 2 2	1 1 2 4	1 1 2 5	1 1 3 3
1 1 4 3	1 1 5 3	2 1 2 1	2 1 2 2	2 1 2 4	2 1 2 5
2 2 2 3	2 3 2 3	2 4 2 3	2 5 2 3	3 1 1 3	3 1 3 3
3 1 4 3	3 1 5 3	3 2 2 3	3 3 2 3	3 4 2 3	3 5 2 3
4 1 1 3	4 1 2 1	4 1 2 2	4 1 2 4	4 1 2 5	4 1 3 3
4 1 4 3	4 1 5 3	4 2 2 3	4 3 2 3	4 4 2 3	4 5 2 3
5 1 1 3	5 1 2 1	5 1 2 2	5 1 2 4	5 1 2 5	5 1 3 3
5 1 4 3	5 1 5 3	5 2 2 3	5 3 2 3	5 4 2 3	5 5 2 3

VII. Simulation Results

To evaluate the performance of the Anti-Mind algorithm, we made an exhaustive simulation over all possible secret codes, with 1000 runs for each secret code. In this simulation, the computer is the codemaker and the codebreaker. In Figure 1 we show the distribution of runs by the number of guesses to find the secret code. Then we repeat the simulation maximizing the number of repetitions of each guess. In Figure 2 we show

Algorithm 2 Second version of Anti-Mind with feedback

$flag\_not\_found \Leftarrow 1$
$n\_digits \Leftarrow$ input('Number of Digits=')
$dig\_max \Leftarrow$ input('Maximum Digit=')
$secret\_code \Leftarrow generate\_s\_c(n\_digits, dig\_max)$
$counter \Leftarrow 0$
while $flag\_not\_found$ **do**
  $counter \Leftarrow counter + 1$
  $guess \Leftarrow input('Guess =')$
  $cpc \Leftarrow calc\_cpc(secret\_code, guess)$
  $cpe \Leftarrow calc\_cpe(secret\_code, guess)$
  $cpc\_o(counter) \Leftarrow cpc$
  $cpe\_o(counter) \Leftarrow cpe$
  $guess\_o(counter) \Leftarrow guess$
  if $cpc = n\_digits$ **then**
    display('You Found It')
    break
  end if
  for i=1:counter-1 **do**
    if $1 - flag\_bad\_guess\_o(i)$ **then**
      $cpc\_i \Leftarrow calc\_cpc(guess, guess\_o(i))$
      $cpe\_i \Leftarrow calc\_cpe(guess, guess\_o(i))$
      $flag\_bad\_guess \Leftarrow 1 - (cpc\_i = cpc) + 1 - (cpe\_i = cpe)$
      if flag_bad_guess **then**
        break
      end if
    end if
  end for
  $flag\_bad\_guess\_o(conter) \Leftarrow flag\_bad\_guess$
  if flag_bad_guess **then**
    display('Bad Guess!')
    in=input('Do you want to see the good guesses?')
    if $in == 1$ **then**
      combination=zeros(1,n_digits)
      $flag\_end \Leftarrow 0$
      while 1-flag_end **do**
        for i=1:counter-1 **do**
          $cpc\_i \Leftarrow calc\_cpc(combination, guess\_o(i))$
          $cpe\_i \Leftarrow calc\_cpe(combination, guess\_o(i))$
          $flag\_coher \Leftarrow 1 - (cpc\_i = cpc\_o(i)) + 1 - (cpe\_i = cpe\_o(i))$
          if flag_coher==0 **then**
            break
          end if
        end for
        if flag_coher **then**
          display(combination)
        end if
        $combination \Leftarrow gen_next\_comb(combination)$
        $flag\_end \Leftarrow all\_combs(combination)$
      end while
    end if
  end if
  $flag\_not\_found \Leftarrow 1 - (cpc = n\_digits)$
end while

the results of this simulation. Comparing the two figures, we can say that the results of the second simulation are worse than the results of the first simulation, since we have a greater percentage of runs with 5 guesses. This way we can say that playing mastermind *well*, with repetitions, has a lower performance than the Anti-Mind algorithm performance. So we confirm that the computer *thinks* better than the human [2].

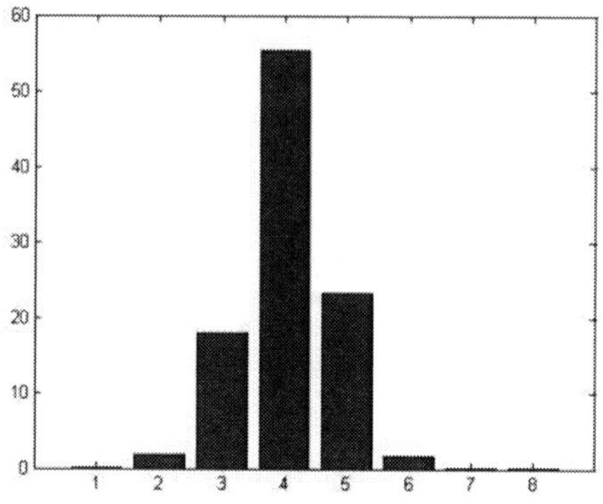

□

FIGURE 1. NUMBER OF GUESSES IN PERCENTAGES DISTRIBUTION OF THE ANTI-MIND ALGORITHM.

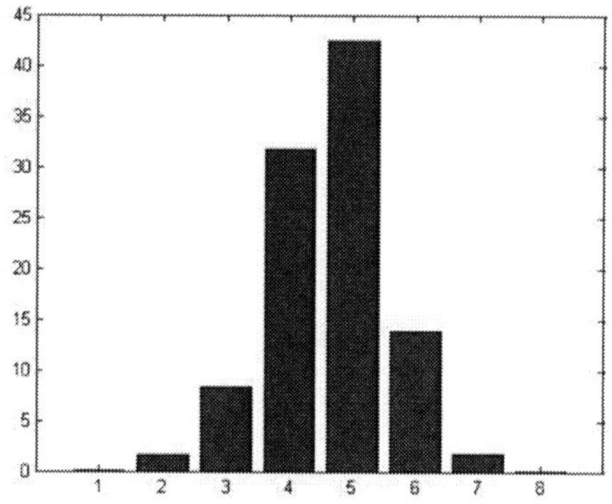

FIGURE 2. NUMBER OF GUESSES IN PERCENTAGES DISTRIBUTION OF THE ANTI-MIND ALGORITHM WITH MAXIMIZATION OF REPETITIONS OF GUESSES.

VIII. CONCLUSIONS AND FUTURE WORK

We showed how to define rigorously what it is meant by playing Mastermind well and how the Anti-Mind algorithm can be used to learn playing well, resulting in the Anti-Mind with feedback algorithm. In the near future, we plan to demonstrate the five hypotheses enunciated in this work as theorems.

REFERENCES

[1] "Games Gift Guide," Games and Puzzles, vol. 20, pp. 16-17, December 1973.

[2] J. Barahona fa Fonseca, "Anti-Mind and Anti-Mind with Feedback: an Example where the Computer Thinks better than the Human," Proc. Congress in Cognitive Neurosciences, University of Evora, Nov. 2003, pp. 55-61.

[3] D. E. Knuth, "The Computer as Mastermind," Journal of Recreational Mathematics, vol. 9, 1976, pp. 1-6.

[4] V. Chvtal, "Mastermind," Combinatorica, vol. 3, 1983 pp. 325-329.

[5] M.M. Flood, "Mastermind Strategy," Journal of Recreational Mathematics, vol. 18, 1985, pp. 194-202.

[6] M.M. Flood, "Sequential Search Sequences with Mastermind Variants-part 1," Journal of Recreational Mathematics, vol. 20, 1988, pp. 105-126.

[7] M.M. Flood, "Sequential Search Sequences with Mastermind Variants-part 2," Journal of Recreational Mathematics, vol. 20, 1988, pp. 168-181.

[8] J. Barahona da Fonseca, "The Anti-Mind with Unlimited Number of Lies as a First Step to Detective Reasoning Modeling," Proc. ICIEIS 2014 Conference, ICIEIS Press, Nov. 2014, pp. 200-205.

APPENDIX

Enough Information Games with 8 Guesses

```
>> anti_mind_real(4,5,1, 1)
Number of Possible Good Guesses=1296
move 1=0111
cpc=0
cpe=1
Number of Possible Good Guesses=308
move 2=1222
cpc=1
cpe=0
Number of Possible Good Guesses=90
move 3=1333
cpc=1
cpe=0
Number of Possible Good Guesses=20
move 4=1444
cpc=0
cpe=1
Number of Possible Good Guesses=6
move 5=4320
cpc=2
cpe=2
Number of Possible Good Guesses=3
move 6=4302
cpc=1
cpe=3
Number of Possible Good Guesses=2
move 7=4023
cpc=1
cpe=3
**ENOUGH INFORMATION**
move 8=4230
**You Found It! in 8 Guesses, with 0 bad Guesses and 0 hints **

Number of Possible Good Guesses=1296
move 1=2201
cpc=0
cpe=2
Number of Possible Good Guesses=222
move 2=5320
cpc=3
cpe=0
Number of Possible Good Guesses=8
move 3=5322
cpc=2
cpe=0
Number of Possible Good Guesses=7
move 4=5520
cpc=2
cpe=0
Number of Possible Good Guesses=4
move 5=5310
cpc=2
cpe=0
Number of Possible Good Guesses=3
move 6=4320
cpc=3
cpe=0
Number of Possible Good Guesses=2
move 7=0320
cpc=3
cpe=0
**ENOUGH INFORMATION**
move 8=3320
**You Found It! in 8 Guesses, with 0 bad Guesses and 0 hints **

Number of Possible Good Guesses=1296
move 1=2241
cpc=1
cpe=1
Number of Possible Good Guesses=230
move 2=2532
cpc=0
cpe=2
Number of Possible Good Guesses=34
move 3=5121
cpc=0
cpe=2
Number of Possible Good Guesses=10
move 4=1345
cpc=0
cpe=2
Number of Possible Good Guesses=6
move 5=4254
cpc=1
cpe=0
Number of Possible Good Guesses=3
move 6=3213
cpc=3
cpe=0
Number of Possible Good Guesses=2
move 7=3210
cpc=2
cpe=2
**ENOUGH INFORMATION**
move 8=0213
**You Found It! in 8 Guesses, with 0 bad Guesses and 0 hints **

Number of Possible Good Guesses=1296
move 1=0214
cpc=1
cpe=0
Number of Possible Good Guesses=108
move 2=1111
cpc=0
cpe=0
Number of Possible Good Guesses=81
move 3=0300
cpc=0
cpe=1
Number of Possible Good Guesses=29
move 4=3444
cpc=1
cpe=0
Number of Possible Good Guesses=9
move 5=3232
cpc=3
cpe=0
Number of Possible Good Guesses=4
move 6=3233
cpc=2
cpe=0
Number of Possible Good Guesses=2
move 7=3252
cpc=3
cpe=0
**ENOUGH INFORMATION**
move 8=3222
**You Found It! in 8 Guesses, with 0 bad Guesses and 0 hints **

Number of Possible Good Guesses=1296
move 1=1243
cpc=0
cpe=2
Number of Possible Good Guesses=312
move 2=2551
cpc=1
cpe=0
Number of Possible Good Guesses=50
move 3=3450
cpc=0
cpe=2
Number of Possible Good Guesses=12
move 4=4001
cpc=1
cpe=1
Number of Possible Good Guesses=4
move 5=2024
cpc=0
cpe=1
Number of Possible Good Guesses=3
move 6=0331
cpc=3
cpe=0
Number of Possible Good Guesses=2
move 7=0131
cpc=2
cpe=2
**ENOUGH INFORMATION**
move 8=0311
**You Found It! in 8 Guesses, with 0 bad Guesses and 0 hints **
```

Improved Bi-optimal Hybrid Approximation Algorithm for Monochrome Multitone Image Processing

Rudolf Neydorf
Albert Aghajanyan
Department of Software Computer Technology and Automated Systems
Don State Technical University
Rostov on Don, Russia
Emails: ran_pro@mail.ru, foralbert92@gmail.com

Dean Vucinic
Vesalius College (VeCo)
Vrije Universiteit Brussel (VUB)
Email: dean.vucinic@vub.ac.be
Faculty of Electrical Engineering, Computer Science and Information Technology (FERIT)
Josip Juraj Strossmayer University of Osijek
Email: dean.vucinic@ferit.hr

Abstract– **The paper investigates image tones approximation algorithm for the multitone image processing, which applications examples are in Web development, compression algorithms, machine vision etc. It considers the Monochrome Multitone Image (MMI) approximation of the original palette to be replaced by a palette having significantly less number of tones. For solving such problems, the optimization strategy requires the approximation quality, which maximizes the tones reduction deviation between the original and the approximated images. In particular, such problems are effectively solved with the heuristic Evolutionarily Genetic Algorithms (EGA) fulfilling the required accuracy, while computational costs still remain significant. Thus, this research is focusing on the hybrid algorithm that is combining the heuristic algorithm, in order to provide suboptimal approximation quality, and the deterministic Algorithm of Local Discrete Optimization (ALDO) for finding the local extreme. EGA minimizes the local discrete optimization search area and ALDO guarantees to find the extreme within the search area. In conclusion, such hybrid algorithmic architecture enables the MMI bi-optimization approximation.**

Keywords-heuristic algorithms; evolutionarily-genetic algorithm; image approximation; optimization; hybridization; bi-optimization.

I. Introduction

Image transformation has a wide range of applications. Examples can be found in the art image processing, where the image transformation is used for simplifying the graphical complexity of images by minimizing their file size, which makes their processing faster. Other examples are the recognition algorithms used for finding Objects for Autonomous Navigation (OAN). The goal of this research is to reduce the image palette, which simplifies and makes more efficient the recognition process.

In Technical Sight Systems (TSS) [4], when tracing the safe autonomous navigation route, the encountered objects are recognized by finding their orientation in space, and respective forms. This objective motivates the usage of the Monochrome Multitone Images (MMI). The term «multitone» is introduced to represent the images characteristic, which are defined with pixels of the same color, where each of them has different brightness. Often, the image pixels have different tones of gray color, called improperly «black and white», thus the term «halftone» is found more appropriate to use.

The processing of the real images with a huge number of details is focusing on the raster graphics and this research addresses the Raster MMI (RMMI) approximation.

One of the main properties of any MMI is associated with the Tones Palette (TP). TP is defined as an integer vector of the image tones. The TP properties depend on the TP's size or length, and on the respective TP tones values.

The standard scales are based on the equal tones values distribution. For example, the standard 256-tones palette is defined as the vector: $(0,1,2,\dots 255)^T$. The special purpose scales (which include approximation) can be characterized by a non-equal tones distribution and having different number of tones in the related TP.

The TP size depends on the application domain and the related tones distribution rules depend on the structure of the image tones.

This paper describes the algorithm that transforms the images with large TP size, where each tone is maximized to its respective nearest original, resulting in a significantly smaller TP size, by applying an appropriate tones reduction algorithm. In addition, the computational efficiency is taken into account in order for the solution to be computed as fast as possible.

The rest of the paper is structured as follows. Section II describes the investigation goal and shows the approximation example. Section III presents the fully explained mathematical base of the approximation algorithm. The optimization technology of the developed approximation algorithm, together with the computed experiments, as examples are presented in Section IV. Finally, the conclusions are given in Section V.

II. Problem Formulation

The main goal is to estimate the possibilities of the developed algorithm, which is designed to perform the optimal RMMI approximation, which transforms the Basic Palette (BP) of size n^0, to the RMMI Approximated Palette (AP) of size n^A, as fast as possible.

The optimal 8-tone TP, which approximated the original 256-tones image (Figure 1a), has the following tones distribution structure: (34, 55, 78, 107, 140, 165,

182, 205), as shown in Figure 1b. In Figure 2, the Brightness Frequency (BF) of original (on the top) and approximated image (on the bottom) are shown. The BF structure, shown at the bottom of Figure 2, shows the non-equal tones distribution. This optimum approximation distribution was obtained from the pixels` brightness non-equal tone distribution of the original image (Figure 2, at the bottom). By comparing the images in Figure 1a and 1b, even visually, it is quite easy to conclude that it is not always appropriate to use the big original palette size, as the obstacles recognition is based on the contours found from the image brightness change. Obviously, the application of such reduced palette size simplifies the pattern recognition tasks in such case.

However, it is also obvious that there are various algorithms that can provide such transformation and the difference between them can be found in their implementation complexity and the quality of approximation. The question to be answered is to validate the application of such optimal or suboptimal algorithms when reducing the RMMI palette size.

a) *b)*

Fig. 1. Original image with 256 tones palette (*a*) and transformed image approximated with 8 tones palette (*b*).

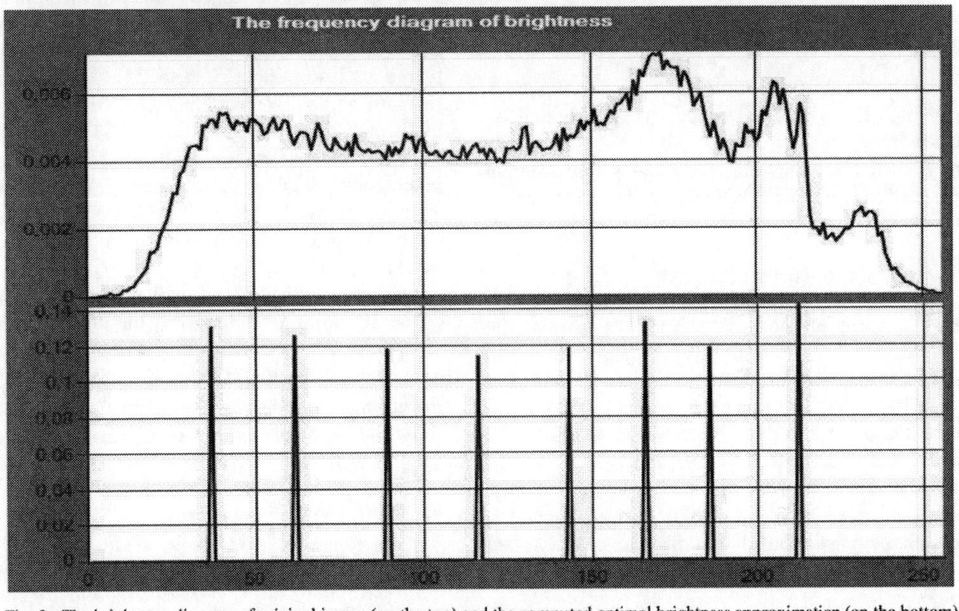

Fig. 2. The brightness diagram of original image (on the top) and the computed optimal brightness approximation (on the bottom)

The investigations have shown that the most effective way to solve the problem is to develop the sub-optimization algorithm, which takes into account the quality of the MMI approximation according to the complexity limits. In other words, the algorithm computing time should allow its practical application. Thus, the goal is to adopt such optimization search for the predefined conditions under the chosen quality criteria in order to achieve acceptable computing time to find extremes.

III. Mathematical Models And Algorithms Of Image Approximation Process

Mathematical model of RMMI. The raster image presents as array of pixels (p). In the rectangle image, the pixels are represented as an ordered array, which is defined by rows i and columns j

$$P = \{p_{ij} \mid i \in [1, r]; j \in [1, c]\}, \quad (1)$$

where r and c – number of rows and columns of pixels that are defined by certain i and j coordinates. The array P can be represented as a rectangle matrix with r rows and c columns:

$$P[i,j] = \begin{pmatrix} p_{11} & \cdots & p_{1i} & \cdots & p_{1r} & \cdots & p_{1c} \\ \vdots & \ddots & \vdots & \vdots & \vdots & \vdots & \vdots \\ p_{i1} & \cdots & p_{ii} & \cdots & p_{ir} & \cdots & p_{ic} \\ \vdots & \vdots & \vdots & \ddots & \vdots & \vdots & \vdots \\ p_{r1} & \cdots & p_{ri} & \cdots & p_{rr} & \cdots & p_{rc} \end{pmatrix}, \quad (2)$$

where in (2) case c>r, which means that it is «widescreen image».

Some RMMI pixels have the same color, but different brightness, called tone. The RMMI palette is defined as the ordered array of (s) tones:

$$B^S = \{b^s | s \in [1, S]\} = (b^1, \dots b^s, \dots b^S). \quad (3)$$

where S – size of the palette, in other words, the number of tones that are used for image display.

Most tasks related to the recognition use RMMI. The ordinary RMMI uses 256 tones of gray color from 0 – absolute black, untill 255 – absolute white, and for each pixel represented with 8 bits ($2^8 = 256$).

Beside the raster image's pixels coordinates i and j, which are determine by (2), there is a need to add a brightness characteristic that define pixel tone. This pixel tone is defined by the index number of s, according to formula (3).

The RMMI's model quantity characteristic (2) is the brightness of pixel with use of its more convenient matrix, the Mathematical Model (MM) of image matrix, where each element is the pixel brightness. The position of each element in matrix (i, j) determines its position in the image rectangle and its number shows the brightness of the certain monochrome image pixel:

$$p_{irs} = b^s. \quad (4)$$

Then, the full MM of the raster monochrome image becomes appropriate to determine the 3-dimensional matrix (or array of 2-dimensional matrices (2) with 3th argument)

$$B^S[i,j,s] = \begin{pmatrix} b^s_{11} & \cdots & b^s_{1c} \\ \vdots & \ddots & \vdots \\ b^s_{r1} & \cdots & b^s_{rc} \end{pmatrix}, \ s = \overline{1,S}. \quad (5)$$

RMMI approximation scheme. The problem of raster image approximation is to reduce the image palette size. Thus, there is a need to decrease the number of tones, which are defining the image. The process consists in replacing the pixels brightness value of the Original Monochrome Multitone Image (OMMI), defined with the Original Palette (OP)

$$B^{S^0} = \{b^0_s | s \in [1, S^0]\} = (b^0_1, \dots b^0_s, \dots b^0_{S^0}), \quad (6)$$

with the brightness values of the approximation palette, whose size is $S^a < S^0$:

$$B^{S^a} = \{b^a_s | s \in [1, S^a]\} = (b^a_1, \dots b^a_s, \dots b^a_{S^a}). \quad (7)$$

The original size of OP S^0 depends on many factors, but primarily is the number of details in the image. The size of the approximation palette S^a can be different and depends only on the approximated MMI application field. For example, in the MS Office Paint editor, only 3 types of colored palettes are available for processing colored image: «24-bit image» (S=2^{24}), «256-colors image» (S=256) and «16-colors image» (S=16). They all defined by formula (3).

The replacement process of image pixels palette (6) to pixels with smaller size palette (7) is called the tone approximation of RMMI. The OMMI transformation result is the Approximated Monochrome Multitone Image – AMMI.

The approximation can be based on significantly different algorithms. However, the underlying basis of all algorithms is the same and consist in changing the pixel tone from OP (6) to the reduced tone AP (7). Also, in OP - B^{S^0} we must define some subarrays of pixels $B^{S^0}_s$, which show the set of pixels that will be covered by one certain pixel from B^{S^a}:

$$B^{S^0}_s \subset B^{S^0}: \forall s \in [1, S^a] \rightarrow \\ \rightarrow \bigcup_{s=1}^{S^a} B^{S^0}_s = B^{S^0} \,\&\, \bigcap_{s=1}^{S^a} B^{S^0}_s = \emptyset. \quad (8)$$

The replacement mechanism of any pixel $b^0_s \in B^{S^0}_s$ to one pixel of AP$b^a_s \in B^{S^a}$:

$$\forall s: b^0_s \in B^{S^0}_s \rightarrow b^0_s \cong b^a_s \in B^{S^a}. \quad (9)$$

Therefore, only 2 factors define the variation and the effectiveness of the algorithm that is converting OMMI to AMMI:

1. Structure of OP dividing on sub arrays $B^{S^0}_s$, in other words, how many and which pixels enter a subarray, where all elements changes their value to b^a_s;
2. Values of b^a_s, where every separate value equals to one of the elements of subarray $B^{S^0} \ni b^0_s = b^a_s$, because the TP values are always natural numbers.

The result of processing a MMI image (4) with any approximation algorithm will result in AMMI, whose MM's structure will be different, because all pixels changed their tone value from OP (6) to smaller size AP (7). If the OMMI's model in palette (6) $P^{S^0}[i,j,s^0]$ contained pixels $p_{irs^0}, s^0 = \overline{1,S^0}$, then AMMI's model will contain p_{irs^a}, $s^a = \overline{1,S^a}$. Thus, every pixel position in AMMI with coordinates (i,j) will be characterized by brightness error:

$$\Delta p_{ijs} = p^a_{ijs} - p^0_{ijs}, i = \overline{1,r}, j = \overline{1,c}. \quad (10)$$

The total error of the image approximation should be calculated based on all AMMI pixels $N = r \cdot c$.

Estimation of monochrome multitone image approximation quality. Using the common form of writing (4) and its variants for OMMI and AMMI in brightness defined form (5) the error for all approximated pixels is defined by the following formula:

$$\Delta b_{ijs} = b^a_{ijs} - b^0_{ijs}, i = \overline{1,r}, j = \overline{1,c} \quad (11)$$

where Δb_{ijs} – resulting deviation, P^A – matrix of approximated image, P^I – matrix of original image and $r \times c = N$ – number of all image pixels.

The difference between the estimation criteria depends on the applied formula for all the image pixels errors.

The investigated question in [13] was to define the most adequate criteria for image approximation. The result was to use the «Least Module of Deviation» (LMD):

$$\Delta_m = \frac{1}{n}\sum_{i=1}^{n}\frac{1}{m}\sum_{j=1}^{m}\left|p^A_{ij} - p^I_{ij}\right| \quad (12)$$

IV. The RMMI Approximation algorithms And AMMI Optimization

A. *RMMI approximation technology*

According to already considered information, the OMMI to AMMI approximation is the sequential execution of the following operations:

1) Chose the size of S^A AP (7);

2) Divide the OP (6) on S^A subarrays $B^{S^0}_s$ (8);

3) Chose S^A tones b^A_s AP from subarray $b^0_s \in B^{S^0}$;

4) Replace sequentially OMMI $N = r \cdot c$ pixels that belong to OP with the nearest to them pixels from AP, which result is AMMI;

5) Evaluate the criteria (12) for AMMI.

To achieve the best possible approximation result, there is a need to organize the algorithm in a way that allows reaching the following condition:

$$\Delta_m\left(B^{S^0}, B^{S^A}\right) = \min_{B^{S^a}} \Delta_m. \quad (13)$$

Thus, it is necessary to realize the algorithm 1-5 as an algorithm for the minimization searching criteria (12). The high resolution of graphical objects (size of AP and number of pixels) motivates developing and using the heuristic Evolutionarily-Genetic Algorithm (EGA). The classic EGA modification on solving the approximation problem showed good accuracy [8], [11], [12] and [13].

B. *The evolutionarily-genetic optimization of AMMI*

It is obvious to consider the RMMI approximation technology (based on the biological mechanism of inheritance). Indeed, if the approximating pixel tones can be selected from OP (6), only then, this palette is equal to a genome, whose elements spawn any AMMI that represents an individual within the approximation algorithm. By following the above approximation technology steps, it is easy to conclude that AMMI-individual, as an image, undoubtedly is determined by the AP structure (7) and the dividing structure OP (7) form sub-arrays. This spawns some clear analogies: (1) between the AP B^{S^a} and chromosome, (2) between the tones b^a_s of AP and genes, (3) between pixels of OP $b^0_s \in B^{S^0}_s$ from subarray, replaced by the tone b^a_s and alleles. All these analogies are providing the variability base for the spawned (by approximation) AMMI.

The first step of the algorithm is the creation of an initial population, which is the random variation of the chromosome alleles (pixels tones of OP within the defined ranges limits). This step allows creating different chromosomes. The individuals of the initial population are estimated according to the criteria from (12). The evaluation results are used to perform «roulette» selection of the population. After the mentioned selection, the population will change under the influence of the genetic operators «crossover» and «mutation», which, as a result, will create the new generation. The convergence of the proposed algorithm is attainment for the last generation.

The described EGA modification is well studied. The difficulties of the EGA application for solving the problems of the dynamic transformation and the image analysis are due to the insufficient computing speed. The needed speed up can be achieved by significantly reducing the population size and the respective number of generations, but, as a drawback, it will sharply decrease the accuracy and confidence level of the computed result.

Another drawback of EGA is the impossibility to estimate the nearness extreme to its optimum. This leads to the increase of the quantity parameters and the time needed to estimate the approximation quality. This motivates the idea to make hybridization between the algorithms of extreme estimation and EGA.

C. *The AMMI extreme estimation algorithm*

The developed deterministic algorithm for any chromosome extreme estimation is based on the genes that represented by natural numbers, which change only on the values that are divided by 1 and have no remainder in the result. This means that the neighborhood of the AP-chromosome (7), as defined at the point in S^a-dimensional space, will consist of the finite number of points, whose coordinates will be deviated from AP tones as 1, -1 or 0. This procedure is illustrated in Table 1.

The central column contains the point coordinates of the 8-dimensional space, for which the extreme has to be found. Any one-element combination in each Table 1 row, with the exception of the combinations of all the elements from the central column, gives a point coordinates in the neighborhood. It is easy to calculate the combinations number as $3^8 = 6561$.

TABLE I. THE EXAMPLE OF NEIGHBORHOOD STRUCTURE OF INVESTIGATED SOLUTION

$b_{ij}-1$	$b_{ij}+0$	$b_{ij}+1$
32	33	34
52	53	54
73	74	75
98	99	100
131	132	133
160	161	162
179	180	181
204	205	206

All these points have to be checked by criteria (12) and, in addition, all the investigated AP points are checked with the condition:

$$\Delta_m\left(B^{S^0},\ B^{S^{A\{e\pm1\}}}\right) > \Delta_m\left(B^{S^0},\ B^{S^{A^e}}\right), \qquad (14)$$

where $B^{S^{A^e}}$ - the AP-chromosome that investigates on extreme, $B^{S^{A\{e\pm1\}}}$ – the array of chromosomes, which are the nearest neighborhood of $B^{S^{A^e}}$. If the condition (14) is satisfied for all elements of array $B^{S^{A\{e\pm1\}}}$, then the found AP solution is at least the local extreme. If there are some points that did not satisfy the extreme condition, then there is a possibility to choose a better point, and in that case, repeat the check. Such possibility motivated a deterministic algorithm creation, which seeks the real extreme in neighborhoods of that point.

It is obvious that the processing time of Extreme Estimation Algorithm (EEA) depends on the AP size. For example, for 8-tone AP, it is necessary to produce 6561 calculations of criteria (12) and check the condition (14). On a computer with the Intel quad 3.3 GHz processor these operations require ~23.85 s. But for 16-tone AP the number of combinations will increase to $3^{16} = 43046721$, which means that the processing time will be 6561 times longer, requiring ~44 hours. Therefore, the application of EEA is only reasonable for small AP sizes. At the same time, the algorithm is quite appropriate for STS, which uses small size palettes.

In such case, it is possible to develop and use the Algorithm of Nearest Extreme Finding (ANEF). The algorithm is based on EEA, with the difference of having a new cycle starting condition, which will be initiated after finding the first AP that is better according to criteria (12) than the investigated one, but simultaneously it has not satisfied the condition (14). The stop condition ending the algorithm will be when the condition (14) is satisfied for the entire AP neighborhood. Therefore, ANEF can be also used as EEA.

Figure 3 shows the protocols of the extreme AP searching steps for the image fragment (Figure 1, displayed by red rectangle) using ANEF from different starting positions. As a result, it takes a different number of steps. However, the last part of the route is the same for all the cases, which can be seen according to equal time to the nearest AP search. In addition, the final extreme check step takes the same time (the small difference is explained by the processor background activity). If the EGA stage is excluded and only ANEF is used as start for the so-called "weighted" distribution [11], [12], then the processing time is 148.7 s.

However, to plan the searching strategy based only on ANEF is not reasonable, because even in this example, it is easy to notice that it depends on the starting position and the computing time can takes 1.5-3 minutes (as shown in this considered case). But, if the AP is provided with criteria value, for example, 415221 (Figure 3), then the time to find the optimum solution will decrease to ~36 s.

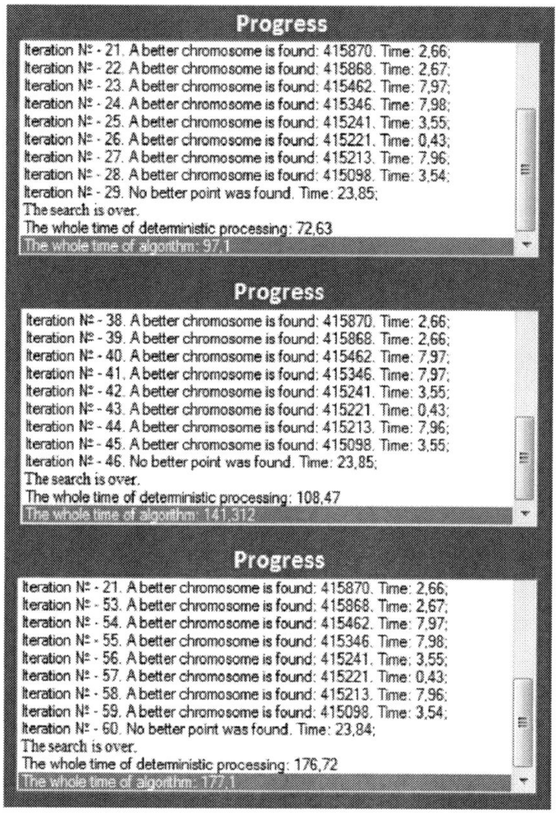

Fig. 3. The ANEF results of the extreme AP search with different starting positions

Therefore, the fair EGA initial setup is to provide a position near to extreme, and to further on apply ANEF, which will check for the solution significantly faster.

For the above-mentioned reasons, it is proposed to use Hybrid Extreme Search Algorithm (HESA), which is based on sequential EGA and ANEF. The results of this research are described below.

D. *The optimization of HESA*

For solving the HESA problem, it is necessary to find such EGA parameters that can find the solution in order for entering the extreme area to be realized within minimal time. These parameters include the number of parallel runs of EGA x_1, size of population x_2 and number of generations x_3.

The 2 Full Factor Experiments (FFE) have been planned and implemented. In the first FFE, the factors variation was on the same low level affecting all the factors: $x_1, x_2, x_3 \in \{2, 4, 6\}$. The results of FFE showed minimal average time (60.7 s.), when all x_i factors had high values. The regression coefficients values were negative for all the linear effects $b_1 = -15.3$; $b_2 = -8.3$; $b_3 = -11.6$.

Because the best FFE average time was too long and the increment observed for all the 3 factors was expected to give significantly better result. The second FFE was implemented with $x_1, x_2, x_3 \in \{4,6,8\}$. And, again, the best average time (47.0 s.) was obtained, when all factors have their maximal values. The regression coefficients give bigger values for the linear effects $b_1 = -18.1$; $b_2 = -17.6$; $b_3 = -12.9$.

The best result of the second FFE is quite near to the maximum faster time of HAES – 23.8 s, which gives the basis for a new investigation – to consider the gradient descent effect. The best result showed that the following parameters $x_1 = 12$; $x_2 = 12$; $x_3 = 10$, give an average time of 40.7 s to obtain the solution. The further EGA's parameters increment increased the computational time, but simultaneously the output result was much nearer to extreme according to criteria (12). The explanation can be found in the EGA processing time. For example, when setting $x_1 = 16$; $x_2 = 20$; $x_3 = 16$, the computational time to find the extreme becomes 544 s.

To summarize, and in accordance with the investigated part of the image, see Figure 1, the most effective solution of the problem was achieved when applying the hybrid algorithm, which is based on the sequential EGA application, with defined parameters, and algorithm of nearest extreme finding.

V. CONCLUSION AND FUTURE WORK

The main research results are:

1. The new developed deterministic Algorithm of Nearest Extreme Finding (ANEF), together with the extreme solution estimation showed to be highly efficient and, thus, it is found to be a very good tool for solving monochrome multitone image tones approximation problems.

2. ANEF became the basis for the hybrid extreme search algorithm, allowing a significant increase in the performance of MMI TP approximation. It enabled the approximation bi-optimization providing the quality estimation with respect to the required computational time.

3. ANEF is the NP full and thus not appropriate for solving the approximation problem, in case of the large TP size needs, which motivates future studies to investigate the possibilities on how to increase the ANEF computational performance.

REFERENCES

[1] J. Puzicha, M. Held, J. Ketterer, "On spatial quantization of color images", *IEEE Transaction on Image Processing*, vol. 9. no. 4, pp. 66-82, 2000.

[2] C. Emre, "Improving the Performance of K-Means for Color Quantization", *Image and Vision Computing*, vol. 29, pp. 260-271, 2011.

[3] Color quantization URL: wikipedia.org/wiki/Color_quantization (date of access: 9.02.2017)

[4] Bishop Ch., "Pattern Recognition and Machine Learning". *Springe*, 2006.

[5] Richard O. Duda, Peter E. Hart, David G. Stork, *Pattern classification*, Wiley, New York. 2001.

[6] D. Chirov, O. Chertova, T. Potapchuk, "Methods of study requirements for the complex robotic vision system", *Spiiran proceedings*, vol. 2(51), pp. 152-176, 2017.

[7] A. Aghajanyan, R. Neydorf, "Optimization of Monochrome Multitone Images approximation based on evolutionarily algorithm", *Omega Science*, Vol.108, pp.11, 2016.

[8] A. Aghajanyan, R. Neydorf, "Optimal approximation of monochrome multi-tone images using the evolutionarily genetic algorithm", *Com-Tech 2016*, pp. 108-112, 2016.

[9] R. Neydorf, A. Derevyankina, "Solving the multiextremal problems with particle swarm method", *Vestnik DSTU*, Vol. 4 (47), 2010.

[10] R. Neydorf, A. Derevyankina, "Solving the recognition problems with particle swarm method", *Izvestiya SFedU*, Vol.7 (108), 2010.

[11] R. Neydorf, A. Aghajanyan, D. Vucinic, "Monochrome Multitone Image Approximation on Lowered Dimension Palette with Sub-optimization Method based on Genetic Algorithm", *ACE-X 2016*, Split (Croatia), 2016.

[12] R. Neydorf, A. Aghajanyan, D. Vucinic, "Monochrome multitone image approximation with low-dimensional palette", *IEEE East-West Design & Test Symposium (EWDTS)*, 2016.

[13] R. Neydorf, A. Aghajanyan, "The research of the application possibilities of tones approximation in a technical vision for the autonomous navigation objects", *Izvestiya SFEDU*, Technical sciences, №1-2 (186-187), pp. 133-145, 2017.

[14] C. Pierre, R. Jean-Philippe, *Stochastic Optimization Algorithms*, Handbook of Research on Nature Inspired Computing for Economics and Management Hershey, 2006.

[15] Vinogradov I., *Mathematical encyclopedia*, Soviet encyclopedia, 1977.

Polynomial Optimization in Mathematical Models Defining Experimental Data Dependencies

Rudolf Neydorf*, Victor Poliakh**
* Don State Technical University,
Russia, Rostov-on-Don,
e-mail: ran_pro@mail.ru

** Don State Technical University,
Russia, Rostov-on-Don,
e-mail : silvervpolyah@gmail.com

Dean Vucinic***
***Vesalius College (VeCo)
Vrije Universiteit Brussel (VUB)
e-mail : dean.vucinic@vub.ac.be

Faculty of Electrical Engineering, Computer Science and Information Technology (FERIT)
Josip Juraj Strossmayer University of Osijek
e-mail : dean.vucinic@ferit.hr

Abstract - **In this paper, the algorithm to mathematically model fragments, which are extracted from non-linear experimental dependencies, is developed, and represents the key steps within the Cut-Glue approximation method. The hybrid search algorithm is based on the classical regression analysis, which takes into account the polynomial structures implemented through the combinatorial laws, and low dimensionality. In the case when the direct search is resource-impossible, the modified evolutionary-genetic algorithm (EGA) is applied. The advantage of the developed algorithm is the guarantee that the optimal polynomial structure exists and can be found. The proposed approach carries out the structural-parametric optimization for each of the studied fragments to define its experimental data dependence. The validation of the polynomial structural-optimization is performed by applying a specially developed software tool, which, in theory, makes possible to approximate fragments of any dimension.**

Keywords – optimization; approximation; regression analysis; mathematical model; experimental data; combinatorics.

I. Introduction

The technical processes occurring in real life are essentially nonlinear and frequently governed by unknown laws [1][2]. Therefore, their direct mathematical modeling is a complex or impossible task, which can be overcome by constructing the Mathematical Models (MM) based on the experimental data, whose input-output dependences are found to be nonlinear [3]. The approximation of such dependencies is a difficult problem to solve and can lead to significant errors, thus special methods are required for effectively solving these problems [4]-[7].

In particular, the presented method is generalized and developed in [8][9]. It is based on the multiplicative "excision" of the modeled dependence sections that are sufficiently and accurately approximated with the analytic functions applying their additive "gluing" characteristics, which allows to have a single analytic function as final result. This data processing approach is called the "Cut-Glue" Approximation (CGA) [5]-[8], and this associative term, in some other related works, is called "multiplicative-additive approximation", as being more mathematically oriented.

The implementation of the CGA method is based on the successive execution of the following operations:

- Cuting out the Experimental Data (ED) array into fragments that can be successfully approximated by appropriate analytic functions (the fragments must have common boundaries, so that their union gives the original array);
- Approximation of fragments by applying the most suitable analytical functions for their data profile to minimize the approximation error and the complexity of the approximation functions;
- Formation of new interval-isolated functions, as different from the functions approximating fragments, which are spatially separated by their coordinate boundaries (special nonlinear multiplicative "cutting" functions [4]-[9] are suggested);
- Assembling the cut-out interval-isolated fragments into a single analytic function (i.e., implementation of the additive operation "glue"), defining the mathematical model of the investigated dependence.

Each CGA method operation determines the quality of the final result. However, the error in the ED mathematical description is, to the greatest extent, determined by the quality of the constructed analytic functions, which isolate the initial experimental data [8][9] that approximates fragments. Therefore, to minimize the approximation error, the received MM can be considered as the key step in the CGA method. This paper is devoted to the development of the methodology and its approximation algorithm, with the focus on the MM regression approximation of data fragments applying the pseudo-linear polynomial combinatorial model. The computed regression polynomial is the approximation function for the applied gene-chromosome model. In addition, the performed computational tests are using the structural-parametric optimization algorithms applying the experimental data regression. The paper goal is to define the analytical function that approximates an arbitrary ED fragment that does not contain any discontinuities in the defined function and its respective derivatives. Such defined dependency function and its structure can be varied and thus, parametrically optimized.

II. REPRESENTING MM REGRESSION APPROXIMATION OF DATA FRAGMENTS BY A PSEUDOLINEAR POLYNOMIAL

Research in the field of the problem, given in [4]-[9], has shown that the method of execution stage approximation fragmented ED treatment should be functionally flexible, combining the flexibility and structure, and analytical and structural diversity. All these requirements are best-served by a well-proven machine classical regression analysis (CRA), focused on the construction of polynomial models [10]-[13]. Polynomial degree has universal design and is suitable for both structural variations within the polynomial members and to effectively optimize the parametric regression coefficients by the method of least squares. As a result, in the polynomial CRA polymer, there is the possibility of effective structural and efficient parametric optimization, which approximates the models for the considered MM fragment.

Structure of Y(x) polynomial of arbitrary m-th degree at the n-th dimension may be represented as follows:

$$Y(x) = b_0 + b_1x_1 + \cdots + b_nx_n + b_{11}x_{12} + b_{12}x_1x_2 + b_{13}x_1x_3 + \cdots + b_{1n}x_1x_n + b_{22}x_{22} + b_{23}x_2x_3 + \cdots + b_{2n}x_2x_n + \cdots + {}_{(n-1)}x_{n-1}x_n + b_{nn}x_{n2} + b_{111}x_{13} + b_{112}x_{12}x_2 + \cdots + b_{11n}x_{12}x_n + \cdots + b_{122}x_1x_{22} + \cdots + b_{1nn}x_1x_{n2} + b_{222}x_{23} + b_{223}x_{22}x_3 + \cdots + b_{22n}x_{22}x_n + \cdots + b_{nnn}x_{n3} + b_{1111}x_{14} + b_{1112}x_{13}x_2 + \cdots + b_{111n}x_{13}x_n + b_{1122}x_{12}x_{22} + b_{1123}x_{12}x_2x_3 + \cdots \quad (1)$$

where $b_{ijk...}$ are the coefficients of the n-th and m-th degree polynomials whose composite indices indicate the variables that are multiplied when forming the polynomial term (for example, b_{1123} is the multiplier for the product $x_1\ x_2\ x_3$); x_i are the indexed independent (input) variables of the experimental dependence being investigated.

One of the simplest and most well-known methods of simplifying the algorithm for finding regression coefficients is the representation of its nonlinear terms as additional arguments of the pseudo-linear factor space of a new vector of variables $\tilde{x}$ of extended dimension, where

$$\forall i = \overline{1,n} \rightarrow \tilde{x}_i = x_i;\ \tilde{x}_{n+1} = x_1 \cdot x_1;\ \tilde{x}_{n+2} = x_1 \cdot x_2;\ \cdots\ \tilde{x}_{n+n} = x_1 \cdot x_n;\ \tilde{x}_{2n+1} = x_2 \cdot x_2;\ \cdots\ \tilde{x}_{3n-1} = x_2 \cdot x_n;\ \tilde{x}_{3n} = x_3 \cdot x_3;\ \tilde{x}_{3n+1} = x_3 \cdot x_4;\cdots\ \tilde{x}_{4n-3} = x_3 \cdot x_n;\cdots, \quad (2)$$

$\tilde{x}_i$ are generalized arguments of the dependency, including the original arguments x_i, and also the pseudo arguments $\tilde{x}_i$, which are all possible products of the original arguments.

In this case, the nonlinear polynomial (1) takes the form

$$Y(\tilde{x}) = \sum_{i=0}^{\tilde{n}} \tilde{b}_i \cdot \tilde{x}_i \quad (3)$$

where bfi_i are the coefficients of the pseudo-polynomial of the $\tilde{n}$-th dimension, b_i and $\hat{b}_i$ - coefficients of any variant of the linear polynomial (3) describing the modeled dependence and are calculated from the well-known matrix formula:

$$\tilde{b} = (X^TX)^{-1}X^TY, \quad (4)$$

where Y is the vector of values of the dependent variable, and X is the matrix of inputs to be examined, which consists of lines $\tilde{x}_i$, the line numbers correspond to the number of the experiment, the column numbers correspond to the term of the polynomial. It is worth noting that the values of the column of conditionally introduced variables $\tilde{x}_0$ of the matrix X are taken in calculations to be equal to unity.

The non-linear polynomial (1) in the form of a pseudo-linear polynomial (3) is well structured, which makes it possible to create a convenient encoding of its terms for computer implementation of combinatorial variation of its structure. This makes it possible to organize a computer search for a structurally and parametrically optimal variant of an approximating polynomial. The need for this is due to the fact that, often, a complete polynomial does not guarantee the best accuracy. This is because the properties of certain nonlinear terms contradict the nature of the approximated dependence. However, which members will be able to describe the model in the best way we do not know in advance. This is due to the peculiarities of the curvature of the hypersurfaces approximating the experimental data of each individual fragment.

III. COMBINATORIAL MODEL OF THE REGRESSION POLYNOMIAL (CMRP)

Form (1) is convenient to organize the successive shifts combinations for the nonlinear terms defined with the polynomial power. In the program, the encoded algorithm mapping is done for a complete multifactor polynomial of any degree using the natural numbers. The increasing series structure is constructed from the indices of its polynomial coefficients and has the following form:

$$0, 1, \dots, n, 11, 12, \dots, 1n, 22, 23, \dots, 2n, \dots, 33, 34, \dots 3n, \dots, nn, \dots 111, 112, \dots, 11n, \dots, 122, 123, \dots, 12n, \dots, 222, 223, \dots, 22n, \dots, nnn, 1111, \dots 111n, \dots \quad (5)$$

The combinatorial analysis of the polynomial structure (5) shows that the number of its variants is determined by the number of combinations of the polynomial terms indices for the variables included in the formula. Consequently, the determination of the structural variants number can be performed using the well-known combinatorial formula:

$$C_k^n = \frac{n!}{(n-k)!k!} \quad (6)$$

where n is the number of independent variables of the polynomial and k is the order of the power polynomial. If the value of C_k^n turns out to be acceptable for calculating all polynomial variants of the selected order within a reasonable time, then the structure-parametric search can be performed by a deterministic algorithm.

Since the algorithm for enumerating all possible combinations of a polynomial is NP, then for the unrealizable value (5) it becomes necessary to use heuristic algorithms for solving this type of problem. In this paper, we use the evolutionary-genetic algorithm (EGA), which is developed as a tool for searching the polynomial terms variation. To find an effective solution, the EGA paradigm is considered in this work, which implies the development of the convenient gene chromosome model for this object-oriented algorithm.

IV. POLYNOMIAL APPROXIMATION FUNCTION FOR GENE-CHROMOSOME MODEL

The essence and originality of the proposed model consists of 2 chromosomes with variable polynomial structure. The main chromosome of the polynomial (meaningful) is given by the sequence of terms of the complete polynomial of the m-th power, ordered by the mnemonic rule (1).

$$Ch=(ch_1, ch_2, \cdots, ch_N) \qquad (7)$$

where N is the number of terms of a complete polynomial of dimension n and of order m.

These terms ch_i ($i = \overline{1,N}$) form the genome of the main chromosome. The binary model is based on the auxiliary (structural) chromosome that forms the structure of the polynomial; its genome is given by a deuce (0, 1). The description of the structure of the polynomial is made by way, where "1" on the next line of the line means using the corresponding polynomial term in the final structure obtained by the merging of the chromosomes. The presence of "0" at some position means the exclusion of this term - the gene of the main chromosome, from the finite structure of the polynomial. In the algorithm, this means that the regression coefficient is considered zero and is not calculated. Thus, the structural chromosome has the form:

$$E = (e_1, e_2, \cdots, e_N), e_i \in (0,1) \qquad (8)$$

With such gene-chromosome scheme for the formation and inheritance of the properties of a polynomial, the mathematical model for the transfer of genetic information from generation to generation is built on a multiplicative basis, and is given by the expression of the following form:

$$P = Ch \cdot E^T \qquad (9)$$

An obligatory condition for such a coding is strict observance of the correspondence between the position of the term in the formula and its structure proposed by the expression (1).

V. SEARCH ALGORITHM FOR OPTIMIZING A POLYNOMIAL APPROXIMATING FUNCTION

The proposed modification of the EGA, like its classic prototype, involves the use of crossing-over operator, mutation and selection. Moreover, the structural chromosome of EGA is used as the transformed chromosome.

The structure of the adjusting parameters of the EGA includes the number of populations, the population size in one generation, the probability of crossing-over and the likelihood of a mutation. At the first stage of the EGA, the initial population is formed, when the mutation operator (Fig. 1a) and single-point crossover are applied to it (Fig. 1b). Further, with the help of the selection operator for each individual received, a decision is made whether to include it or not to include it in the next generation of EGA.

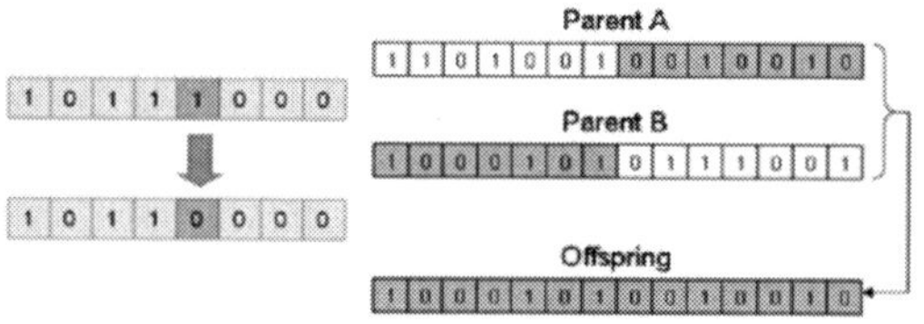

a) b)

Figure 1. Illustration of mutation (a) and crossover (b) operators execution.

The binary chromosomes obtained with the help of crossing-over and mutation operators, which carry the structures information are formulated according to formula (9), where the individuals are defined as the EGA-variants of polynomials.

For selecting the next generation individuals, those already formed, with the repeated polynomial structure, are eliminated with the aid of the EGA. As a result, only the unexplored individuals are passing into the next generation.

The algorithm for calculating the coefficients of linear regression uses the specially developed software.

For the resulting regression equation, the value of the simulated dependence is calculated for the corresponding experimental points, together with the error of the approximating polynomial at each calculated point.

VI. STRUCTURAL-PARAMETRIC OPTIMIZATION ALGORITHMS FOR THE EXPERIMENTAL DATA REGRESSION DESCRIPTION

To obtain the variant, which represents the most accurate sampled data description, the calculated results are ranked in descending accuracy order. Therefore, the first output is the parametric optimum of the problem being solved.

However, there are many results that often satisfy the permissible approximation error. For example, the calculation of all structural variants of a polynomial of order 4 over an array of *m22* defined from 20 experimental data (see Figure 2) leads, according to (5),

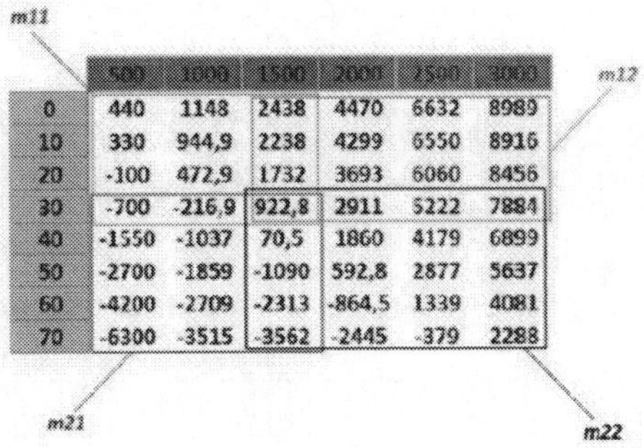

	500	1000	1500	2000	2500	3000
0	440	1148	2438	4470	6632	8989
10	330	944,9	2238	4299	6550	8916
20	-100	472,9	1732	3693	6060	8456
30	-700	-216,9	922,8	2911	5222	7884
40	-1550	-1037	70,5	1860	4179	6899
50	-2700	-1859	-1090	592,8	2877	5637
60	-4200	-2709	-2313	-864,5	1339	4081
70	-6300	-3515	-3562	-2445	-379	2288

Figure 2. The data array of the investigated dependence.

to the receipt of 77,811 solutions. At the same time, from this total number of variants of the polynomial (4), only a few fall under the chosen error limit. Therefore, this is quite accessible for sorting and deciding on the best structural choice by using a conventional PC.

In a particular case, a complete search of all investigated dependence variants is an acceptable approach for identifying the optimal terms combination of the describing polynomial. However, in the case when investigating the large multidimensional dependencies, a full search due to NP-completeness becomes an unsolvable problem. Therefore, it is proposed to solve it with EGA, which performs the suboptimal structure search of the describing polynomial in an acceptable time. However, it cannot guarantee the finding of the optimal polynomial structure.

In this paper, the set of polynomial variants for the 2 approaches is presented, which is characterized both by errors and by structural-parametric estimates of the complexity of the description. For such estimates, different polynomial parameters are considered, such as its order, the total number of its terms, and so on. The regularization of this, largely informal, task is not considered here. The possibilities of this approach are well traced in the example below.

VII. An Example of Applying the Proposed Methods in the Fragments Approximation Optimization.

As an example of the proposed approximation approach, the m22 matrix is examined (see Figure 2), and is defined as a fragment of an experimental data array obtained when describing the dependence of the aerodynamic moment values of an airship with the velocity v and the angle of its roll α taken from [5][6].

At the first stage, the investigated dependence (fragment) is described with the help of a complete 4th order polynomial. Using the classical regression analysis, the coefficients of the polynomial are calculated, from which, by using the obtained coefficients, the analytical estimates of the investigated fragment experimental values for the matrix are found. On the basis of this analytical data and the available experimental data, the regression estimate errors with the greatest relative error for the experimental values are calculated. If the describing relationship accuracy of the complete n-order polynomial is insufficient, the dependence is further investigated by looking through all possible variants of the n-th order polynomial in order to identify the optimal combination of polynomial terms, as well as with EGA.

The total number of variants of polynomial (4) is 21,209, which fulfill the 5% approximation error. The study of the dependence by means of EGA is using the following parameters structure:

Number of individuals in the population = 100

Number of generations = 100

The probability of crossing-over = 60%

Probability of mutation = 30%

Selected approximation error of 5%, for which there are 1059 variants.

When studying the structure by means of the 2 presented methods, it was noted that the data description by the complete 4-order polynomial has the maximum absolute error value of ~ 291.43, and relative error value of ~ 0.0573 (5.73%), which did not fall within the set error limit.

Among the selected variants, the correlation between the complexity of the structure of a polynomial and the approximation accuracy is provided.

In the columns of Table I and Table II, the members of the complete 4th order polynomial appearing in (4) with the corresponding code indicated in the upper line are represented. Their absence is indicated by the symbol "-". The last 2 columns give the maximum estimates for the approximated absolute and relative errors, showing the approximation accuracy for the polynomial variants.

TABLE I. Polynomial structure results by means of EGA

0	1	2	11	12	22	111	112	122	222	1111	1112	1122	1222	2222	Max absolute error	Relative error
0	1	2	11	12	22	111	--	--	--	1111	1112	1122	--	--	47,93095	0,0196
0	1	2	11	12	22	--	--	--	222	--	--	--	--	--	173,10336	0,02196
0	1	2	11	12	22	--	--	--	222	--	--	1122	--	--	178,19125	0,0226
0	1	2	11	12	22	--	--	122	222	--	1112	--	--	--	57,50005	0,02486

TABLE II. POLYNOMIAL STRUCTURE RESULTS BY MEANS OF A COMPLETE COMBINATORIAL SEARCH FOR ALL VARIANTS

0	1	2	11	12	22	111	112	122	222	1111	1112	1122	1222	2222	Max absolute error	Relative error
0	1	2	11	12	22	111	112	--	222	1111	1112	1122	--	--	25,32678	0,0103
0	1	2	11	12	22	111	112	--	222	--	1112	1122	--	--	25,53261	0,0104
0	1	2	11	12	22	111	--	122	222	1111	1112	1122	--	--	26,89585	0,011
0	1	2	11	12	22	111	--	122	222	--	1112	1122	--	--	27,10168	0,0110

Among all the options presented in Table 1, the top row can be considered as optimum, because it has the smallest error. However, despite the fact that the second combination has a large error of about 2%, its structure is more economical than the structure of the first, third and fourth rows. Its combination is the structurally optimal polynomial variant for investigating *m22* dependence (see Figure 2).

In Table 2, the first line represents the best polynomial combination found by means of EGA, which can be considered as an absolute structural parametric optimum, since it has the smallest error for all orders. The second combination has more than 100% greater error and has a more economical structure than the first, but less precise for the data approximation.

For comparing the results of the developed methods, it is worth noting that the results obtained with EGA are not inferior in accuracy to the results obtained by a full search. However, the amount of time that was spent to study the same data structure, in the EGA case is 9 sec, significantly reduce the time of a full search to 65 seconds.

VII. CONCLUSION

This study has shown that the use of different criteria for estimating the accuracy of constructing the regression equation (MNC) and for estimating the accuracy of the mathematical description of data leads to a significant ambiguity between structural complexity and error, which opens the possibility for investigating the solution based on the structural parametric optimization of the created experimental data mathematical model.

The developed algorithm and its respective software implementation make this approach efficient to find the structure and parameters of the suboptimal polynomial variant for the investigated dependence fragment.

It is well known that, when the dimension and the order of the complete polynomial are sufficiently small, the search for all its possible variations is feasible. However, when the dependence dimension and approximation polynomial order increase, finding its best structure by direct selection is not possible, since it is NP-complete. Thus, this identified complexity fully justifies the proposed EGA application in order to make it solvable.

REFERENCES

[1] A. Isidori, *Nonlinear Control Systems, third edition*, Springer Verlag, London, 1995.

[2] H. K. Khalil, "Nonlinear *Systems", third edition*, Prentice Hall, Upper Saddle River, New Jersey, 2002.

[3] R. Neydorf, and Y. Sigida, "Identification of Traction and Power Characteristics of Air-Screw Propulsors in Mathematical Description of Airship,", SAE 2014 Aerospace Systems and Technology Week, September 23 – 25 2014 – Cincinnati, OH, USA// SAE Technical Paper 2014-01-2134, 2014.

[4] R. Neydorf "Approximation building of mathematical models by experimental data with using of "Cut-Glue" method", Vestnik DSTU, 2014, T14, № 1 (76). - pp. 45-58.

[5] R. Neydorf, "Cut-Glue Approximation In Problems On Static And Dynamic Mathematical Model Development", Proceedings of the ASME 2014 International Mechanical Engineering Congress and Exposition, Montreal, Quebec, Canada, November 14-20, 2014.

[6] Neydorf, R., "Bivariate "cut-glue" approximation of strongly nonlinear mathematical models based on experimental data," SAE International Journal of Aerospace, № 1, vol. 8, 2015, pp.47-54, doi:10.4271/2015-01-2394.

[7] R. Neydorf and A. Neydorf "Technology of Cut-Glue Approximation Method for Modeling Strongly Nonlinear Multivariable Objects. Theoretical Bases and Prospects of Practical Application," SAE Technical Paper, 2016, doi:10.4271/2016-01-2035

[8] R. Neydorf, I. Chernogorov, V. Polyakh and O. Yarakhmedov "Formal Characterization and Optimization of Algorithm for the Modelling of Strongly Nonlinear Dependencies Using the Method "Cut-Glue" Approximation of Experimental Data", SAE Technical Paper, 2016, doi:10.4271/2016-01-2033.

[9] A. Sen and M. Srivastava, "Regression Analysis — Theory", Methods, and Applications, Springer-Verlag, Berlin, 2011.

[10] D. Serber, "Linear regression analysis" Mir, 1980, pp. 450-456.

Optimal Design of Diffuser and Matching Lens in Proton Radiography

Haibo Xu
Institute of Applied Physics and Computational Mathematics, Beijing, China
e-mail: xu_haibo@iapcm.ac.cn

Qinggang Jia
Institute of Applied Physics and Computational Mathematics, Beijing, China
e-mail: 345515962@qq.com

Abstract—**In this paper, we study the optimal design of diffuser and matching magnetic lens in high-energy proton radiography. The constraints related to the limitation of overall length, maximum magnetic lens intensities, cross-sectional size of magnetic lens and the size of object are all addressed using the genetic algorithm. The parameters of the diffuser and the matching lens are obtained to be suitable for the proton beam of 20 GeV. The Monte Carlo code Geant4 is applied to verify the diffuser performance and to improve it.**

Keywords-proton radiography; multiple Coulomb scattering; diffuser; matching lens.

I. Introduction

Compared to X-ray, high-energy protons perform better as a radiographic probe for dense objects in hydrotest experiments because of their extremely penetrating power [1]. The three most important effects on the protons as they go through an object are absorption, Multiple Coulomb Scattering (MCS), and energy loss. The MCS effect will seriously blur the radiographic image of the object. To suppress this kind of blurring, a magnetic structure called Zumbro lens was developed by Mottershead and Zumbro [2].

The protons that are not scattered or absorbed in the object emerge from the object with a reduced energy spread due to collision with atomic electrons. The energy spread, together with chromatic aberration in the lens, causes image blurring. Chromatic aberrations in the magnetic lens can be minimized by making the lens system as short as possible and by using an illuminating beam with a special correlation between transverse position and angle. The protons must have an "angle-position correlation", which means that the angle of the illuminating rays is a linear function of the distance from the axis, as if it comes from a (virtual) point source a distance upstream of the entry plane of the lens. Before entering the imaging lens that forms the radiographic images, the proton beam passes through a thin tantalum sheet, which spreads the beam so it can illuminate the entire test object. The beam passes through a set of quadrupole electromagnets that gives the protons the angle-position correlation. The matching lens may give the protons the necessary correlation [3].

To the best of our knowledge, there is no report on how to design both the diffuser and the matching lens. Some references [4-6] focus on optimal design of Zumbro lens (downstream of matching lens). These designs are mainly based on an analytic method with thin-lens approximation. With all constraints such as Fourier points and Field-of-View (FOV) [4], the allowed parameter sets can produce the inverting identity (-I) magnetic optics. Beam physics packages such as MARTLIE [5] and COSY [6] are employed to compute the chromatics for each parameter set. Regarding the design of the diffuser and the matching lens, several constraints such as the position-angle correlation required by Zumbro lens, FOV size and drifting length are limiting the searching of best solutions with less chromatic aberration. This kind of chromatic aberration is produced when the proton attenuates the diffuser. So, the design of both the diffuser and the matching lens is expected to be a multi-objective optimization with many constraints. Therefore, we employ genetic algorithm (GA) as the optimization method because it is recognized as the best globally well-adapted optimization algorithm [7]. The Monte Carlo code Geant4 is applied to verify the diffuser performance [8].

This paper is organized as follows. The principles of the diffuser and the matching lens are presented in Section II. In Section III, the numerical results are obtained with the GA. Finally, the conclusion is given in Section IV.

II. Principles of Diffuser and Matching Lens

The designed matching lens should have two functions. The first function is to provide proton beam with the desired angle-position correlation at the object plane. The second function is to expand the beam size to fully illuminate the object. In addition, the design should consider the upstream diffuser. The diffuser works together with the matching lens. Once the lens is designed, the thickness of the diffuser is obtained. To get a lower chromatic aberration, a thinner diffuser should be used. However, if the diffuser is too thin, it may not provide the required position-angle correlation for the matching lens. Therefore, the diffuser thickness should also be taken into the matching lens optimization.

The transfer of a proton in matching lens of x plane has the form:

$$\begin{pmatrix} Ax_0 \\ wAx_0 \end{pmatrix} = \begin{pmatrix} M_{11} & M_{12} \\ M_{21} & M_{22} \end{pmatrix} \begin{pmatrix} x_0 \\ w_0 x_0 + \varphi_{\text{diffuser}} \end{pmatrix} \quad (1)$$

Here, A is the amplification factor of matching lens; w is the required correlation at the object plane; w_0 is the correlation when the proton is at the entrance of the matching section;

φ_{diffusr} represents all deviations from the correlation line due to both MCS in the diffuser and non-zero emittance in the illuminating beam; M is the x plane transfer matrix of the matching lens. The value of w_0 is not only involved in the matching lens, but it also closely relates to the diffuser.

Compared to the distance from matching lens to the diffuser, the beam size is small. The proton beam is approximated as a point source. Therefore, w_0 equals to the reciprocal of the draft from the diffuser to the matching lens D_1. Then, w_0 is expected to have a positive correlation with the diffuser thickness:

$$w_0 = \frac{1}{D_1} \propto T_{\text{diffusr}} \tag{2}$$

To decrease the chromatic aberration caused by the diffuser, a thin diffuser should be used. However, it results in a large distance between the matching lens and the diffuser. Therefore, apart from the correlation and amplification, a reasonable value of w_0 should be carefully selected in the optimization of the matching lens.

If the φ_{diffusr} is close to zero, then (1) can be expressed as

$$\begin{cases} M_{11} + w_0 M_{12} = -A \\ M_{21} + w_0 M_{22} = -wA \end{cases} \tag{3}$$

The equation for y plane is similar to (3). If w is positive in the x plane, it is equal in magnitude and negative in the y plane. Equation (3) acts as the constraints in the optimization.

The design of the diffuser and matching lens is expected to be a multi-objective optimization. The traditional method is based on thin-lens approximation. It takes the size of field of view (FOV) as a posterior limitation on the parameters. However, this may not provide the best solution. The constraints should be taken as object functions to guarantee a reasonable result. The GA is recognized as the best globally well-adapted optimization algorithm and this is why we decided to use it in our approach.

III. OPTIMIZATION FOR PROTON RADIOGRAPHY

The basic structure of both the diffuser and the matching lens can be found in Figure 1 (trajectories are simulated by Geant4 code [8]). The matching lens consists of three quadrupoles combined with four drifts. The proton beam starts from the right side and it is scattered by a diffuser. Then, the beam with angular divergence drifts (with length of D_1) to the matching lens with position X_0 and direction vector w_0*X_0 in x-axis. When the proton transport to the end of matching lens has position A*X_0 and direction vector A*w_0*X_0 in x-axis, then the beam will cover the object.

The goal of the optimization is to obtain a higher amplification factor of the matching lens. The parameters to optimize are drifts: D_1, D_2, D_3, D_4, the magnetic lens thicknesses: T_1, T_2, T_3 , magnetic lens strength G_1, G_2, G_3 and diffuser thickness. The constraints are related to the limitations of overall length, maximum magnetic lens intensities, cross-sectional size of magnetic lens and the size of object. Because w_0 can be calculated by drift length D_1, the domain of w_0 is set to be from 0.1 to 0.13 to ensure an available drift length. The GA is employed to obtain a matching lens with larger amplification.

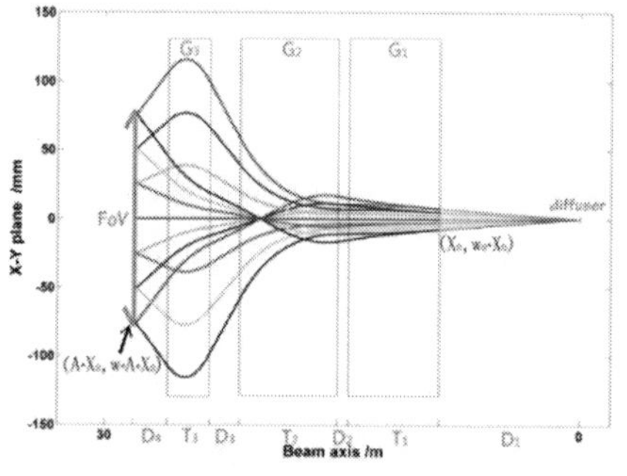

Figure 1. Simulated proton trajectories in matching lens.

All the constraints can be written as:

$$\begin{cases} \sum_{i=1}^{4} D_i + \sum_{j=1}^{3} T_i \le 27 \\ G_i \le 10, i = 1,2,3,4 \\ \left| X_{\text{pos}} \right| < \min(R_{\text{quadrupoles}}, R_{\text{drift\_tube}}) \\ R_{\text{FOV}} > R_{\text{object}} \end{cases} \tag{4}$$

in which the $R_{\text{quadrupoles}}$ and $R_{\text{drift\_tube}}$ are the inner radius of quadrupoles and drift tubes, X_{pos} is the proton position value on the designed trajectories. This constraint means the proton should not bombard the magnet. The R_{FOV} is a function of A and diffuser thickness.

The matching lens should provide the proton beam with the necessary correlation for Zumrbo lens, which means the vaule of w in (3) is fixed. With constraints shown in (3) and (4), the object is to minimize the difference between the obtained w and the desired Zumbro lens. All the constraints could be written as a penalty term which is part of the object fuction. The contribution of each constraint can not be expressed by a formula. Therefore the optimizer may use intelligent optimization algorithms.

For the proton beam of 20 GeV , we use GA and found the best results are obtained when: the drifts D_1=7.95m, D_2=0.70m, D_3=1.90m, D_4=2.00m; the magnet length T_1=5.72m, T_2= 6.17m, T_3=2.65m; the field gradient G_1=1.00T·m^{-1}, G_2=9.93 T·m^{-1}, G_3=8.79T·m^{-1}; diffuser thickness T_{diffuser}= 1.50mm.

Two issues should be noted for the parameters. (2) is obtained by using the assumption which the initial beam comes from a point source. Therefore, $1/w_0$ is just an initial value of D_1. Geant4 is employed to obtain the exact value of D_1 by repetition simulations. The secondary issue is relevant to the thickness of the diffuser.

If the parameters of the required proton beam are obtained, the diffuser thickness can be calculated. To use the proton beam efficiently, the proton intensity at the center of illuminating beam should be higher than that at the edge of FOV. The root mean square (RMS) angular deviation θ_0 induced by the expected diffuser can be calculated by:

$$\varphi_{\text{diffusr}} = \sqrt{\theta_0^2 + \varphi_0^2} = \sqrt{\frac{\theta^2}{-2\ln[I(\theta)/I(0)]}} \qquad (4)$$

where φ_0 is the angular deviation of the beam generated by the accelerator. θ_0 is the MCS angle given approximately by

$$\theta_0 \approx \frac{14.1\,\text{MeV}}{pc\beta}\sqrt{\frac{T_{\text{diffusr}}}{X}} \qquad (5)$$

Here, p is the beam momentum, $\beta = v/c$ where v is the beam velocity and c is the speed of light, and X is the radiation length for the material of the diffuser.

Combining (4) with (5), the thickness of tantalum diffuser can be obtained.

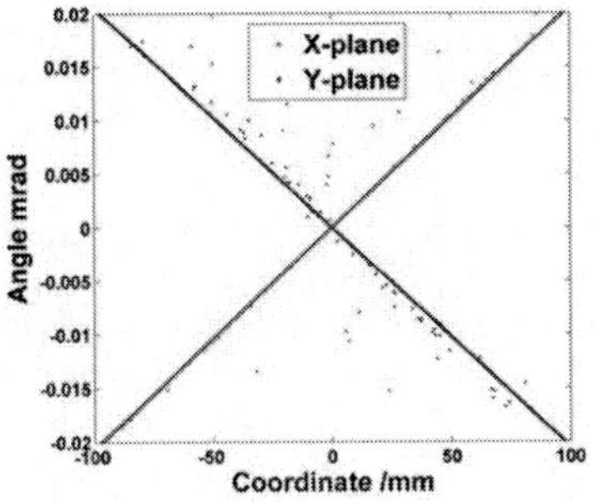

Figure 2. The angle-positon correlations at object plane.

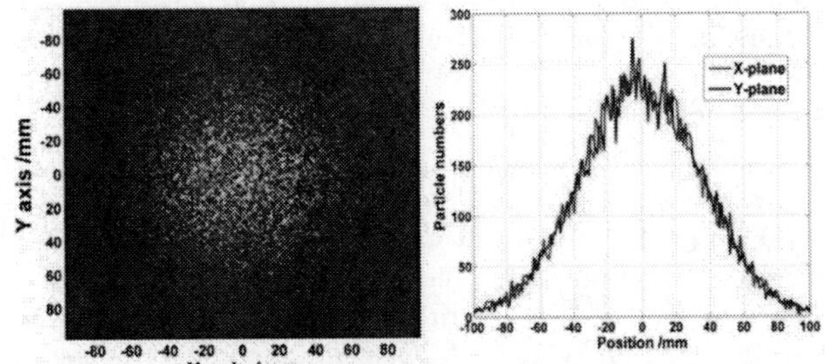

Figure 3. The planar distribution and cross-sectional distribution profile at the object plane.

The designed diffuser, matching lens and Zumbro lens were assembled as a whole system and simulated by Geant4. The obtained angle-position correlations for both x and y planes at the object plane are given in Figure 2. The simulated correlations coincide with the design. The simulation also shows that over 95% of protons can pass through this whole system, and finally reach the detector.

Figure 3 shows the beam distribution at the object plane. The result shows that the proton flux at the edge of FOV is about 20% of the maximum value. The beam distribution is also consistent with our design. Both the diffuser and the matching lens work as expected.

IV. CONCLUSIONS

The diffuser and matching lens are key components in high-energy proton radiography. In order to minimize chromatic aberration, the optimal design of the diffuser and matching lens should provide the proton beam with the necessary correlation for Zumrbo lens imaging system. The domains of parameters, magnification, target size and the thickness of diffuser are all considered by the genetic algorithm. The parameters of diffuser and matching lens are obtained for the proton beam of 20 GeV. The beam distribution is consistent with our design by use of the Monte Carlo code Geant4. Thus, the study is beneficial for the design of the magnetic lens in high-energy proton radiography.

REFERENCES

[1] C. L. Morris, J. W. Hopson, and P. Goldstone, "Proton Radiography," Los Alamos National Laboratory, LA-UR-06-0331, 2006.

[2] C. T. Mottershead and J. D. Zumbro, "Magnetic Optics for Proton Radiography," Proc. Particle Accelerator Conference. Vancouver B C, 1997, pp. 1397-1402.

[3] A. J. Jason, "Magnetic Imaging Lenses for the Advanced Hydrodynamic Facility," Los Alamos National Laboratory, LA-UR-00-5447, 2000.

[4] Y. M. Antipov, et al., "A Radiographic Facility for the 70 GeV Proton Accelerator of the Institute of High Energy Physics," Instrum. Exp. Tech., vol. 53, 2010, pp. 319-326.

[5] F. E. Merrill, et al., "Magnifying Lens for 800 MeV Proton Radiography," Review of scientific Instruments, vol. 82, 2011, pp. 103709.

[6] H. Y. Barminova and V. I. Turtikov, "Proton Microscope Design for 9 GeV pRad Facility," Journal of Instrumentation, vol. 11, 2016, pp. 05021.

[7] M. Zbigniew, "Genetic Algorithms+Data Structures= Evolution Programs," Springer, Berlin, 1999.

[8] S. Agostinelliae, et al., "Geant4 –a Simulation Toolkit," Nucl. Instrum. Methods Phys. Res. A, vol. 506, 2003, pp. 250-303.

An Interactive Learning Tool for Teaching Sorting Algorithms

Ahmad R. Qawasmeh, Zohair Obead, Mashal Tariq, Motaz Shamaileh, Ahmad Shafee

Department of Computer Science
The Hashemite University
Zarqa, Jordan
Email: ahmadr@hu.edu.jo, zjaj.zm2006@gmail.com, mashalalmomani@yahoo.com, motazsh81@gmail.com, shafii4ever@gmail.com

***Abstract*—Sorting is a crucial process for managing data and it is used in many scientific fields. This paper presents a learning interactive tool that helps students to efficiently understand the concepts, design, and techniques of sorting algorithms. We developed a user-friendly Web application, based on some multi-media elements such as graphics interchange format, to describe the working process of different sorting algorithms in a simulation-based way. Six common sorting algorithms that include Bubble sort, Quick sort, Merge sort, Radix sort, Insertion sort, and Selection sort were implemented, analyzed, and demonstrated in this application. Our application simplifies the learning process of algorithms by giving the user an interactive and animated way for analyzing and understanding the design of sorting algorithms in a detailed manner. Based on a conducted study, the results of using our tool demonstrated an average improvement of 40% in the grades of students in the course "Introduction to Algorithms" compared with the students, who did not use this tool in two previous semesters. The tool also increased the students' motivation and willingness to take this course.**

Keywords*–*Algorithm visualization; Performance analysis; E-Learning; Sorting algorithms; Simulation tools.

I. INTRODUCTION

In mathematics and computer science, an algorithm is a step-by-step set of operations to be performed on specific input(s) to achieve specific output(s). Algorithms preform calculations, data processing, (and/or) automated reasoning tasks.

Due to the massive growth of modern learning methods, it has become easier to simplify the difficulty and complexity of computer operations related to algorithms, where the ability to view items visually is available in the modern software. The visual explanation of algorithms speeds up the process of understanding certain things that might need to be explained in detail. Different previous studies conducted in the teaching methods field argue that some students in Computer Science face difficulties understanding the abstract concepts of programming [1][2].

In this work, we came up with an idea of designing an educational application that provides visual elements and detailed explanation for six different sorting algorithms commonly used in computer science. The application offers a suitable environment for users (students and instructors) interested in the sorting algorithms field and an ability to simplify the learning process of how these algorithms actually work. Our application provides an interactive way for face to face and distance learning, detailed visual representation and simulation about the covered algorithms, convenient and friendly user interface, and easy way to electronically update the material of the course.

The main motivation of this work lies in the following points:

- Instructors need to have an interactive tool to deliver information to students of higher educational levels.
- Students need, rather than traditional books whether they are paper or electronic, an interactive system, which allows them to interact with the material so as to achieve the educational goal and makes learning interesting and exciting.
- The algorithm courses are based on experimental visual explanation. This fact makes the usage of visible elements and tools for delivering information a necessity.
- Sorting algorithms are based on different design paradigms and techniques. It is important to develop a tool that can visually depict the similarities and differences between these techniques in order to understand the drawbacks of using one algorithm over the other.

Figure 1 shows the main components of the proposed tool.

This paper is organized as follows. Section 2 discusses the related work. Section 3 describes the methodology and implementation. Section 4 presents our results and finding. Finally, Section 5 concludes our contributions and mentions directions for the future work.

II. RELATED WORK

Different Web applications [3]-[4] perform a visual way to simulate the process of sorting inputs in sorting algorithms. They provide an interactive environment to improve the ability to deliver information. The user can interact with the Web page to see how the algorithm works and how the process of sorting is virtually done. ALGAE [5] allows C++ or Java code to produce a simulated version of that code. Marcelino et al. [6] developed a tool that can be used to support initial stages of programming learning using a procedural approach. Krushkov et al. [7] provides a tutoring system for programming. Some of these applications only cover numeric values and ignore the other types of data. In our application, we simplified the design to improve users interaction with the application and developed an easy to use application with explanation about every algorithm.

Some other applications focused on analyzing how some of the most popular sorting algorithms work [8] [9]. These

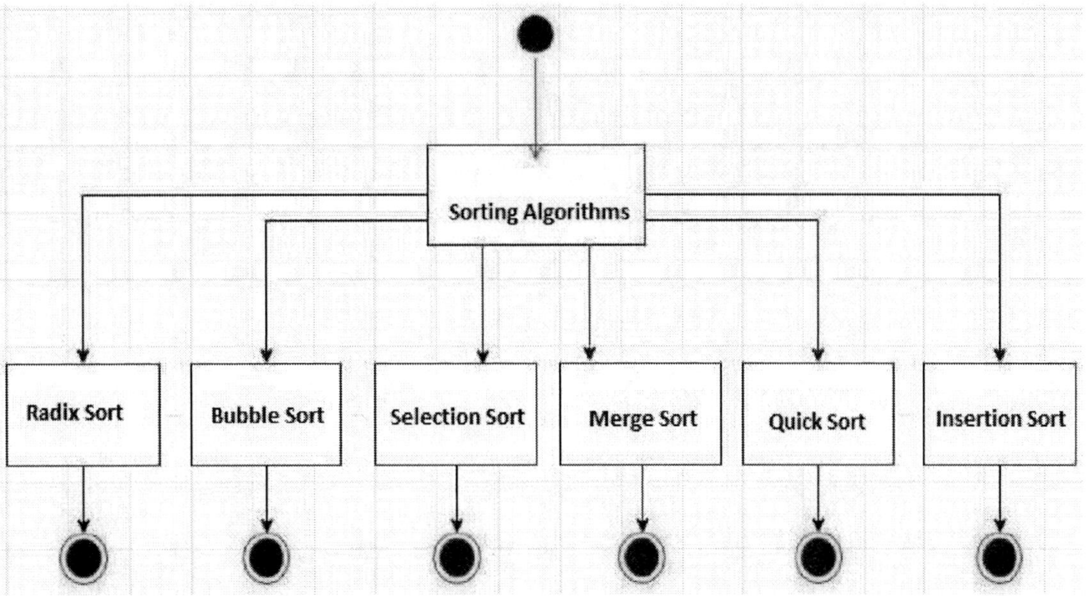

Figure 1. Components of the developed tool

applications provide two standpoints to look at algorithms: one is artistic, and the other is more analytical aiming to explain algorithms step by step. In contrast, our tool focuses on explaining how sorting algorithms work from a learning point of view.

In terms of teaching, Tuparov et al. [10] [11] developed and used an interactive simulation-based Learning Objects in an introductory course of programming focusing on sorting algorithms. Their study showed an increase in students' willingness and understanding. However, the main drawback of this work was the limited number of sorting algorithms, which were covered. TRAKLA2 [12] is a framework, which was developed for building interactive algorithm simulation exercises. Exercises constructed in TRAKLA2 are viewed as learning objects in which students manipulate conceptual visualizations of data structures in order to simulate the working of given algorithms. Grivokostopoulou et al. [13] presented an educational system that assists students in learning and tutors in teaching search algorithms. Automatic assessment was achieved in four stages, which constitute a general assessment framework. On the contrary, our tool focuses and covers a sufficient variety of sorting algorithms implemented via different design techniques.

On the other hand, Hundhausen et al. [14] presented a systematic meta-study of 24 experimental studies to examine the effectiveness of algorithm visualization in education. Their most significant finding was that how students use algorithm visualization technology has a greater impact on effectiveness than what algorithm visualization technology shows them. We worked on this finding in our tool by showing students how to use the tool efficiently to gain the most outcome. More details about the use of our tool are given later in the paper.

As can be obtained from the aforementioned discussion, our tool provides a sufficient variety of sorting algorithms, which covers both comparison and non-comparison based algorithms. In contrast, most of the current tools discuss comparison-based sorting algorithms only, especially when the tool is related to an introductory algorithms course. Moreover, our tool provides an easy interactive way, which motivates students and users to become more engaged with the topic of sorting algorithms.

There are other tools and applications that have been developed and used in the context of algorithms. However, we tried to focus on the most recent and relevant researches.

III. Methodology and Implementation

Because of the importance of design in any Web application, we tried to create an attractive and flexible interface that provides a convenient way of interaction for students/instructors. In other words, user can easily access our application and choose the type of sorting he/she wants to explore. Our system responds by giving the user an animated way to learn how the chosen algorithm sorts the input data, while displaying the algorithm's pseudo-code and observing the current variable values.

In our application, we used Hyper Text Markup Langaue (HTML), Cascade Style Sheet (CSS) and Java-script to design the front-end environment, while using Personal Home Page (PHP) for implementing the back-end functions and methods. For animation, we used the canvas library for the process of moving objects on the screen, then we added the corresponding algorithms to the animation code to create a simulation environment.

A. User Interface

The home page of our tool is divided into separate frames reachable easily by the user. By clicking on the "ALGORITHMS" tab, the algorithms page, shown in Figure 2, will be displayed. This page consists of six different algorithms.

Each sorting algorithm page has an explanation paragraph that gives the user an overview of the algorithm. We also inserted a graphic multimedia element, as shown in Figure 3 to give the user a visual explanation about the algorithm. At

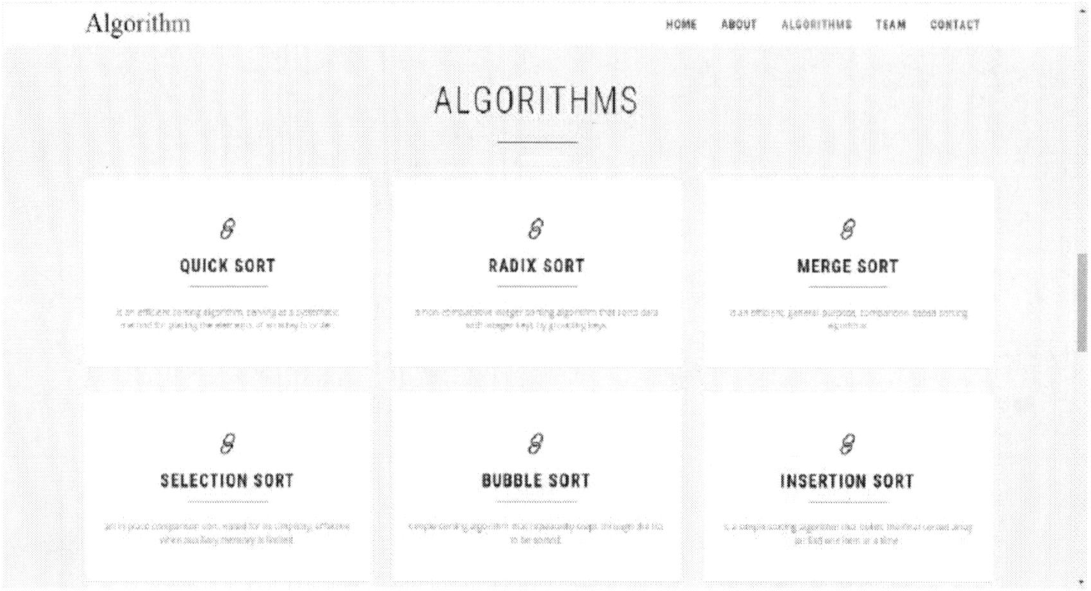

Figure 2. Sorting algorithms main page

the bottom of each page, we created a link, which transfers the user to the animation page.

For animation, we designed attractive simulation pages for each implemented algorithm. From a technical point of view, user can insert his own values or try the random numeric values given by the tool. After inserting the values and clicking on the sort button, the tool will start sorting the values according to the chosen algorithm. The tool gives the user a code tracker (pseudo-code) to make the process of understanding more efficient, while displaying the current variables values. The pseudo-code also describes the design paradigm used.

Figure 4 demonstrates the simulation process of the Quick sort algorithm. Each color assigned to the displayed bars has its own meaning depending on the used algorithm, and this is thoroughly explained in every algorithm page. The same animation format was used in all comparison-based sorting algorithms, demonstrated in our tool, that include bubble sort, selection sort, insertion sort, and merge sort. However, we developed another animation format for the non-comparison Radix sort algorithm, as shown in Figure 5. We included this type of sorting to help instructors explain the difference between comparison-based and non-comparison based sorting algorithms to their students more attractively.

The tool also has an input/output page that can track a flat file containing unsorted data. The tool returns the values sorted. This page can track any value type (numeric, character, string, etc.) and produce a file with sorted data. The output file can be downloaded to the local directory of the users computer.

New algorithms can easily be added to our learning tool, as the simulation environment has already been developed. We first need to modify the home page to add the corresponding new algorithm. Second, we need to add a graphic multimedia element page to give the user a visual explanation about the new algorithm. For animation, we just need to add the corresponding algorithm to the existing animation code.

B. A study for observing the efficiency of the tool

Our tool consists of the most popular algorithms: Bubble sort, Selection sort, Merge sort, Radix sort, Quick sort, and Insertion sort. A study was conducted in the undergraduate course "Introduction to Algorithms" in the college of Information Technology at the Hashemite University in Jordan on a sample of 100 students. This sample includes students in their second, third, and fourth academic year. The students of our sample also have different high school background, where two high school sections (1- Science 2- Information Technology) were considered. This variety in our sample ensures the correctness and accuracy of our findings. The main idea of this study was to compare the average grades of these students with the grades of students from two previous semesters, in which this tool was not available. We compared the results with two previous semesters, rather than one, to increase the accuracy and reliability of our study. The tool was available to students for self-learning and was also used during the face to face lectures and office hours. The instructor demonstrated the simulation with different input data to show students how to obtain the best case, average case, and worst case of each algorithm, while explaining the changes of colors and values of variables.

IV. Results

Our observations through the conducted study performed in the "Introduction to Algorithms" course demonstrated promising results. The use of our simulation-based tool as an alternative to the traditional way of explaining algorithms was really efficient and reliable. First of all, the students were impressed by the use of the interactive tool. The element that was the most interesting to them was the ability to observe the behavior of every algorithm, while changing the input data. The students had the chance to understand the impact of input data on the complexity of algorithms. The students also managed to implement the pseudo-code of these

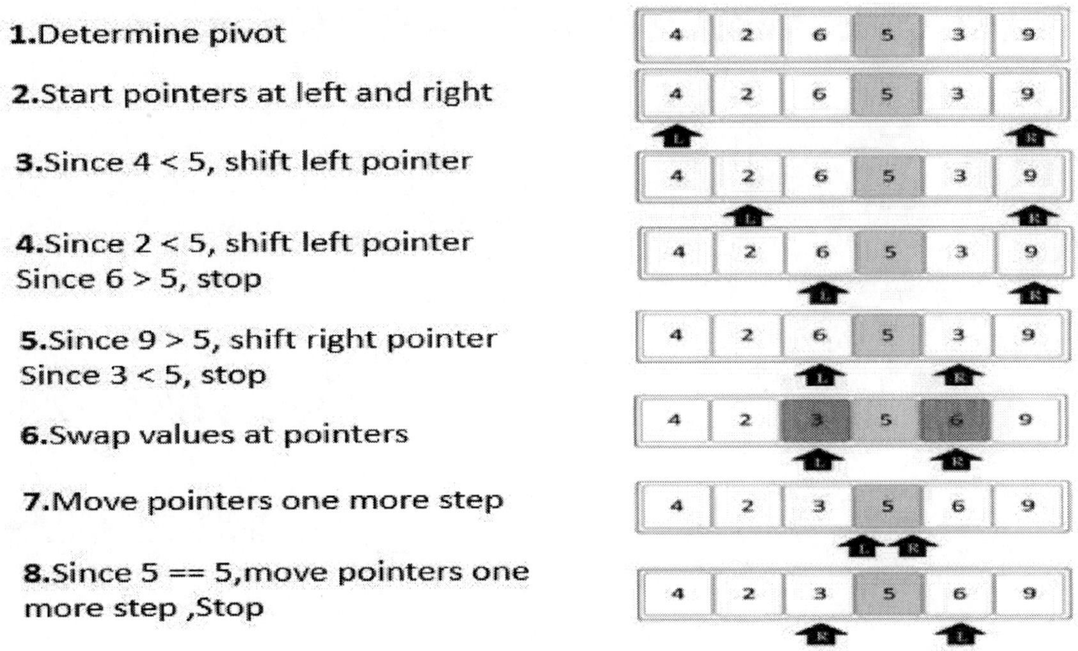

Figure 3. Quick Sorting multimedia page

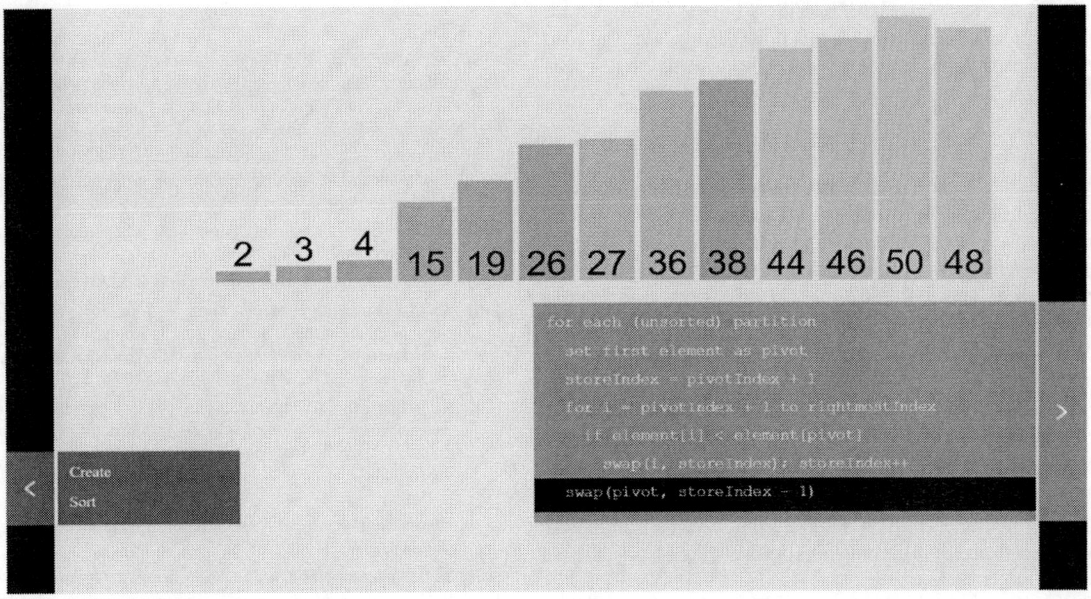

Figure 4. Quick Sorting animation page

algorithms more easily using different programming languages such as java or C++. The simulations of algorithms also helped the students to understand the different design paradigms used to implement the covered algorithms and how they can be adopted to implement other algorithms. The percentage of students participating in the discussions during lectures significantly increased compared with the previous semesters, in which the simulation-based tool was not used.

Furthermore, the grades of the current students were significantly better than the students who took the course previously without using the tool. The results demonstrate an average improvement of 40% in the grades of students in the exam covering the sorting topic in the course "Introduction to Algorithms" compared with the students who did not use this tool in two previous semesters. More students are also interested in taking this course in the summer semester based on the observations from the initial registration period.

At the end of next semester, we plan to conduct a survey,

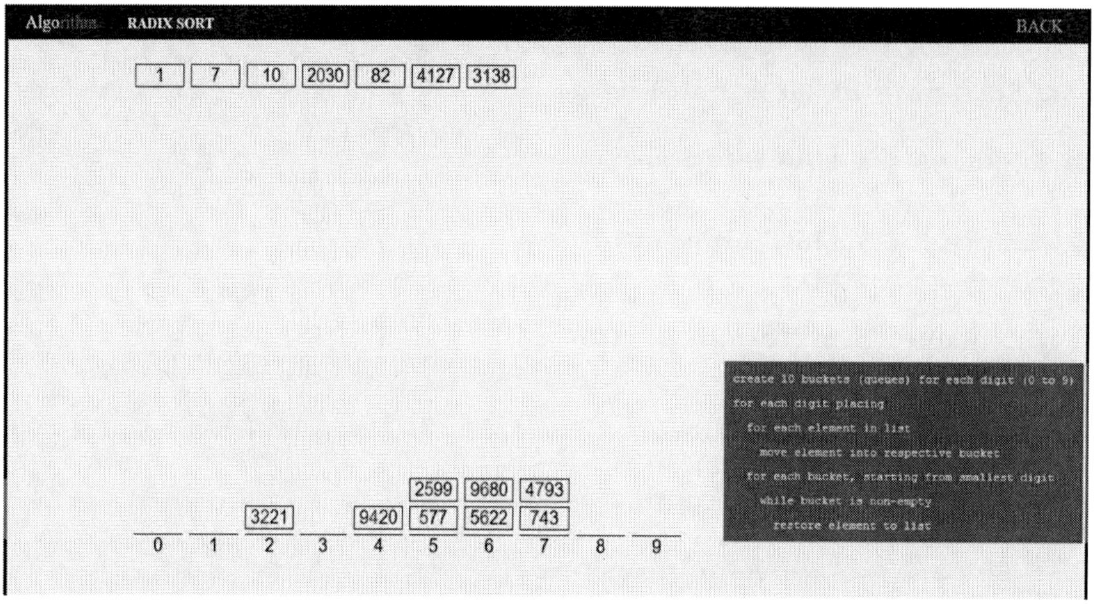

Figure 5. Radix Sorting animation page

directed to students, to have a better idea about using the simulation-based tool in teaching. This shall be an important step to get students' feedback about how to improve the tool and if it is useful to simulate other algorithms that solve different problems.

V. Conclusions and Future Work

The application proposed in this paper was designed as a learning tool that can be used by instructors/students to facilitate the process of teaching sorting algorithms. The tool provides an interactive environment and meets the requirements of modern learning. The tool has an animated explanation for the process of sorting via different sorting algorithms that vary in terms of usage, design technique, best/worst case running time complexity, and concept. The tool is compatible with different browsers and can handle different input data types. Last but not least, the tool demonstrated promising results based on a conducted study performed on a sufficient sample of students.

Path forward, we plan to simulate the working process of other algorithms depending on a survey that will be conducted soon. We also think that making this tool available on mobile phones will improve learning.

Acknowledgment

The authors would like to thank the Hashemite University for providing the required resources.

References

[1] C. M. Areias, A. J. Mendes, and A. J. Gomes, "Learning to program with proguide," in Proc. Int. Conf. Engineering Education, 2007.

[2] G. Rößling, "A family of tools for supporting the learning of programming," algorithms, vol. 3, no. 2, 2010, pp. 168–182.

[3] visualgo.com, "Algorithm Visualisation," http://visualgo.com, 2017, accessed: 01-01-2017.

[4] University of San Francisco, "Sorting visualization, comparison sorting algorithm," http://cs.usfca.edu, accessed: 13-11-2016.

[5] Steven J. Zeil, "AlgAE (Algorithm Animation Engine)," http://www.cs.odu.edu/~zeil/AlgAE/referenceManual.pdf, 2011, accessed: 13-11-2016.

[6] M. Marcelino, T. Mihaylov, and A. Mendes, "H-sicas, a handheld algorithm animation and simulation tool to support initial programming learning," in Frontiers in Education Conference, 2008. FIE 2008. 38th Annual. IEEE, 2008, pp. T4A–7.

[7] H. Krushkov, M. Krushkova, V. Atanasov, and M. Krushkova, "A computer-based tutoring system for programming," Mathematics and Mathematical Education, 2009.

[8] Aldo Cortesi, "Sorting Algorithm Visualisation," http://sortvis.org, 2010, accessed: 13-11-2016.

[9] Carlo Zapponi, "Sorting," http://soting.at, 2014, accessed: 13-11-2016.

[10] G. Tuparov, D. Tuparova, and V. Jordanov, "Teaching sorting and searching algorithms through simulation-based learning objects in an introductory programming course," Procedia-Social and Behavioral Sciences, vol. 116, 2014, pp. 2962–2966.

[11] G. Tuparov, D. Tuparova, and A. Tsarnakova, "Using interactive simulation-based learning objects in introductory course of programming," Procedia-Social and Behavioral Sciences, vol. 46, 2012, pp. 2276–2280.

[12] L. Malmi et al., "Visual algorithm simulation exercise system with automatic assessment: Trakla2," Informatics in education, vol. 3, no. 2, 2004, p. 267.

[13] F. Grivokostopoulou, I. Perikos, and I. Hatzilygeroudis, "An educational system for learning search algorithms and automatically assessing student performance," International Journal of Artificial Intelligence in Education, vol. 27, no. 1, 2017, pp. 207–240.

[14] C. D. Hundhausen, S. A. Douglas, and J. T. Stasko, "A meta-study of algorithm visualization effectiveness," Journal of Visual Languages & Computing, vol. 13, no. 3, 2002, pp. 259–290.

Modbus-A: Automated Slave ID Allocation Enabling Architecture for Modbus Devices on RS485/232

Bharath Sudev*#, Iain Kinghorn*, Dongbing Gu#, Doug Gower*

* Fläkt Woods UK
Colchester, England CO4 5ZD
Email: {bharath.sudev, iain.kinghorn, doug.gower}@flaktgroup.com

School of Computer Science and Electronic Engineering
University of Essex, Colchester, England CO4 3SQ
Email: {bs16733, dgu}@essex.ac.uk

***Abstract*—If Modbus devices are to be connected on to the same communication infrastructure, each device must be powered up individually and manually given a unique ID. This can be a time-consuming and laborious process if the system has a plurality of devices. This paper presents the architecture, implementation and testing information of Modbus-A, an architecture that allows the master device on a communication infrastructure to autonomously set the IDs of live devices, which are already connected to the bus. Furthermore, the concept is validated using a software simulator as well as using a hardware prototype.**

Keywords*— *Modbus; Modbus-A; autonomous Modbus ID allocation.

I. Introduction

Modbus [1] is a single master multiple slave protocol. As per the specification, the master should be connected to the slaves in a daisy chain topology, as shown in Figure 1. The slave devices will have unique slave IDs, using which the master will address them during communication.

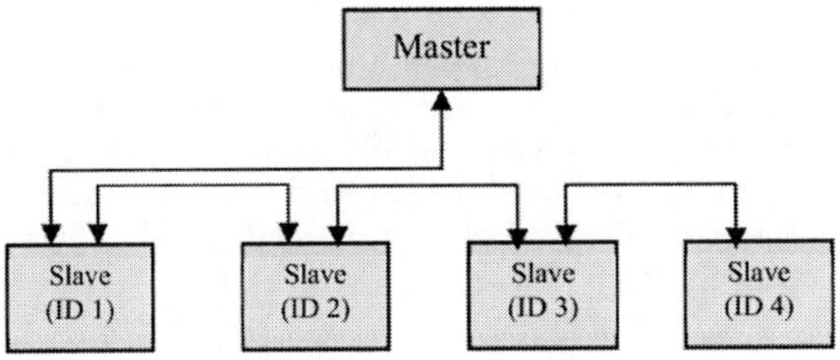

Figure 1. Normal multi slave operation

To get information from a slave or to set a parameter on the slave, the master sends a message with the slave ID through the daisy chain. As an example, if the master sends a message with the ID=3, the slaves with ID1 and ID2 will ignore the message and forward it down the chain. When the slave with its ID set as 3 receives the message, it will process the instruction and send a response message through the chain back to the master.
However by default, Modbus devices out of the box typically will have an ID of 1. So, one would not be able to connect devices out of the box into a daisy chain topology as there will be multiple devices with the same slave ID of 1, as shown in Figure 2.

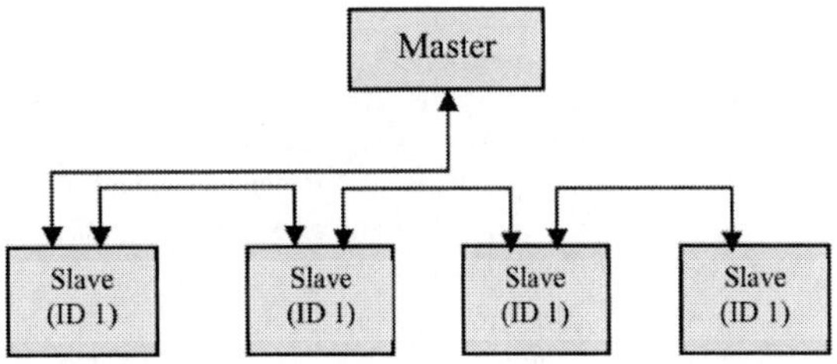

Under such a situation, the devices will have to be disconnected, powered up individually and given unique slave IDs individually before connecting them into the daisy chain. This can be a time consuming and difficult process when there are a wide number of devices. It is even harder in situations where the devices are already installed and needs reconfiguration.

This paper will present Modbus_A architecture along with the implementation and test result of our patent pending (GB2017008577) concept that will enable automatic reconfiguration of slave IDs of devices which are already in a daisy chain.

This paper is organised as follows. Section II presents related work on Modbus communication followed by the architecture and functionality of Modbus-A in Section III. Section IV presents information on software simulation conducted and its results. Section V then presents the hardware implementation followed by conclusion as Section VI.

II. Related work

Modbus is a protocol widely used in industrial devices like inverters, sensors and control systems. As previously mentioned, every message from the Modbus master will have a slave ID in it to designate the intended recipient of the message.

Followed by the slave ID, the master will send a function code specifying the requested operation followed by some data (if required) and error check code. The frame format of a Modbus message is shown in Figure 3.

Figure 3. Modbus frame format

Though every slave in the system will receive each message, only the slave with the same address (ID) as in the message will accept the message while the other slaves ignore it. On reception of the message, the slave will do the requested operation and respond with a message back to the master containing its slave ID as a confirmation. If the master fails to receive a confirmation message, the master will retransmit the message as the pervious message is assumed to be lost [2]. So, it is critical that the slaves have unique Modbus IDs lest multiple slaves will attempt to reply to the master's message simultaneously thereby failing the protocol. Since the devices typically will have a Modbus ID of 1 out of the box, there will be duplication of IDs on the bus if there are multiple devices.

In such a situation, each must be powered up separately and given a unique Modbus ID before connecting them to a common communication medium. The difficulty of setting the ID will increase with the number of devices and the location of its deployment.

Naismith et. al. [3] present a concept where the master device polls through all the possible address in the network on start-up. This enables detection of devices on the network if all of them have unique Modbus IDs. However, this is a time-consuming process and would not work if there are devices with same Modbus IDs.

Liang et. al. [4] present a concept that will enable reconfiguration of slave IDs when there are ID conflicts. The system employed slaves with unique identification numbers in them. In case of devices with conflicting Modbus IDs, the master requests the conflicting slaves to send their unique identification number to the master within a certain pre-set interval like in Ethernet [5]. The slaves then will attempt to send their ID back after a random waiting period so that the IDs are received at the master reliably. In case the IDs are not received by the master, the same process will be re-initiated several times until the identification numbers of all the slaves are received. Once the identification numbers of the slaves are received successfully by the master, the master will then send configuration messages to set Modbus ID of each slave referring to it by its identification number. Since the technique relies on each slave having its own unique identification number, there could be difficulty in adopting this as a universal standard as use of different types of devices or devices from different manufactures can result in duplication of identification numbers on the network. Furthermore, in a system with many slaves, the master will have to send multiple retransmission messages to the slaves; and the slaves will have to attempt to respond with its identification number multiple times per message from the master for a successful transmission. So, the configuration time will increase significantly with the number of devices on the communication infrastructure.

A similar concept is presented in [6] where the master initially will send a broadcast message to retrieve Modbus IDs of all the devices on the network. This technique also involves the use of a unique identification number in the slave to enable communication to devices with same Modbus slave IDs.

In case of ID conflicts, the master will request the slaves with conflict to send their Modbus IDs combined with their unique identifier thereby formulating a total ID. To prevent conflicts of reply messages, each slave will delay the message back to the master for a time period proportional to its total ID. Due to the use of unique identifiers on the slaves, this technique could also suffer from the limitations as with [4] as discussed previously. A similar approach is seen in [7] where the slaves are identified using unique identifiers and communication is possible either using Modbus or TCP (Transmission Control Protocol).

On the contrary, Lloyd [8] presents a concept that enables slave devices to send unsolicited messages to the master requesting identification/configuration. Successful transmission of the message is ensured by using principles used in Ethernet like Address Resolution Protocol [9] and Dynamic Host Configuration Protocol [10]. On receipt of the message, the master is able to allocate ID to the device. This technique is thus able to resolve ID conflicts by using complex logic on the slaves which enables unsolicited messages transmission using certain protocols. This paper presents the Modbus-A protocol that enables resolution of ID conflicts using a computationally light method with minimal overheads.

III. MODBUS-A ARCHITECTURE AND FUNCTIONALITY

Modbus-A slaves have two ports for communication. The slaves have two states of operation, a default state where the two Modbus ports are connected internally using a Modbus bridge as in Figure 4(a) and configuration mode where the Modbus bridge is disconnected, as shown in Figure 4(b).

(a) (b)

Figure 4. Modbus-A slave modes
(a) Default mode (b) Config mode

As a result, Modbus-A slaves will function as any other traditional Modbus slave under normal operation, as shown in Figure 5.

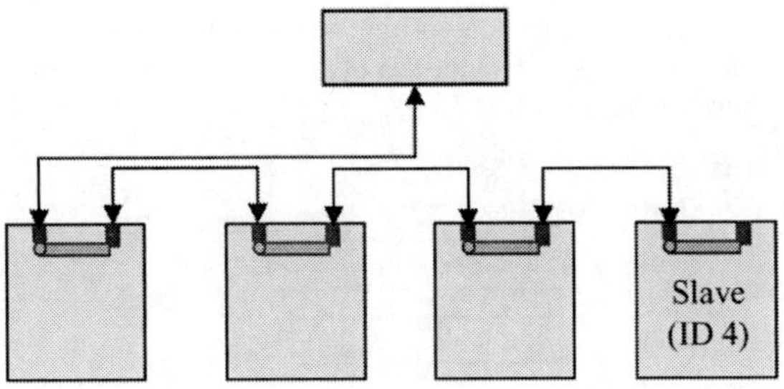

Figure 5. Normal multi slave operation

Consider the condition where the slaves are new out of the box and hence have ID=1, as shown in Figure 6.

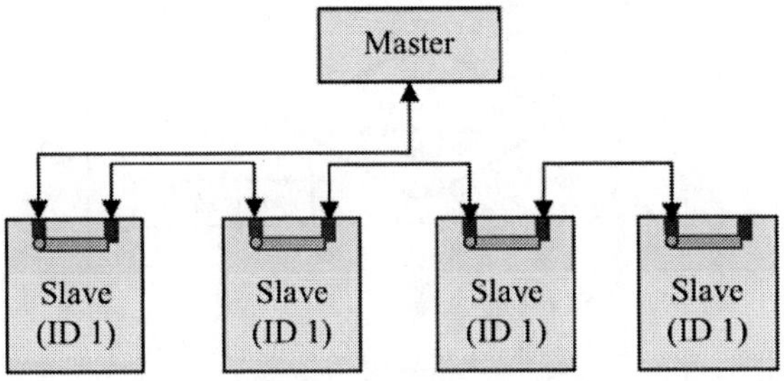

Figure 6. Configuration out of the box

To make the system work, the slaves must be set with unique IDs. With Modbus-A, the master can be made to do this automatically in two stages as explained below.

A. *Reset stage*

The master sends a reset message to the daisy chain. Regardless of the slave ID, every device that receives the message will accept it and transmit it to the next slave. Once the message is transmitted to the next device, each slave will switch to configuration mode thereby disintegrating the daisy chain by opening the Modbus bridge, as shown in Figure 7. The slaves will also clear their own slave ID. After sending the reset message the master switches to re-config stage.

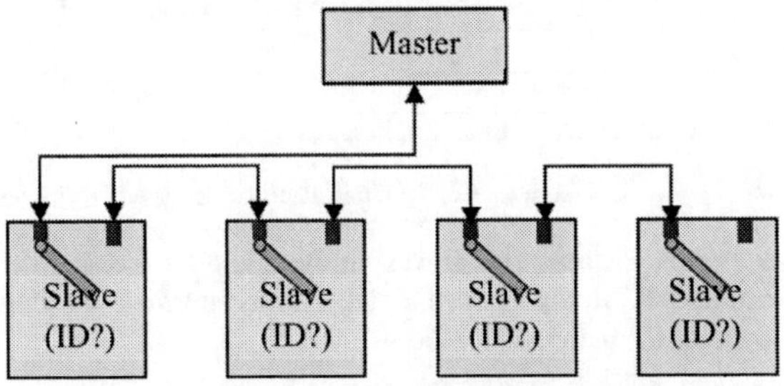

Figure 7. Auto-reconfiguration sequence step 1

B. *Re-config stage*

In re-config stage, the master sends messages with incrementing slave ID so that the slaves which are in configuration mode can set its ID and go into default mode. In the example in Figure 7, the master first sends a configuration message with ID=1.

Since the slaves are in configuration mode and hence have disconnected Modbus bridges, only the first slave will receive the message. On receiving the message, the slave will set its ID to 1 and then change its mode to default, as shown in Figure 8. On setting the slave ID, the slave will send an acknowledgement message to the master thereby confirming the configuration.

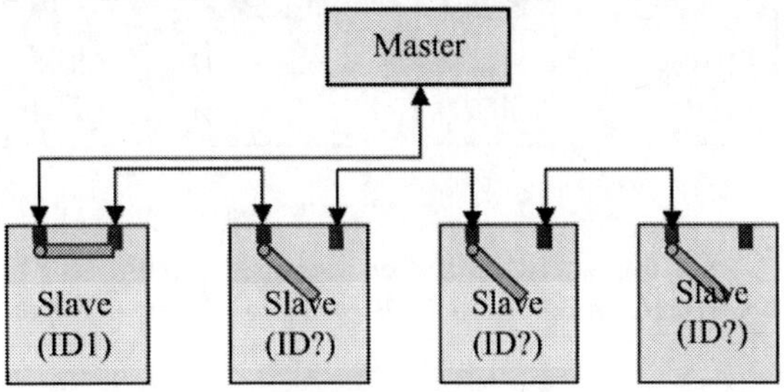

Figure 8. Auto-reconfiguration sequence step 2

As the master is in the re-config mode, it will keep on sending configuration messages with unique slave IDs using an incrementing counter. So, the second message from the master will have an ID of 2. Since the first slave in the example already has a slave ID (of 1) and is in the default mode, it will ignore the message and transmit it to the second slave.

Since the second slave is in configuration mode, it will set its ID in accordance with the ID in the message and switch to normal mode without transmitting the message to the next slave. This is shown in Figure 9. The slave will also send an acknowledgement message back to the master.

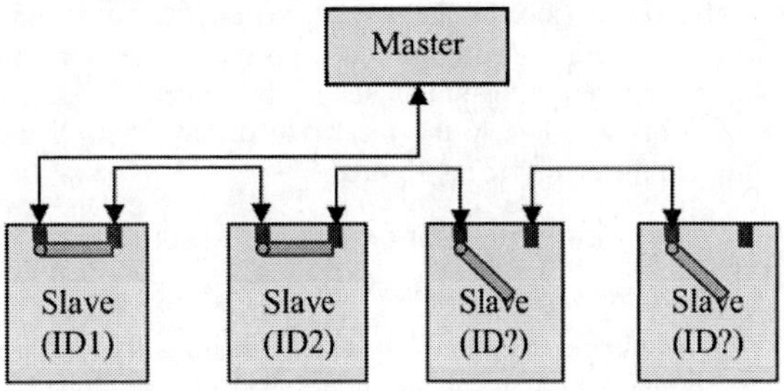

Similarly, the third message from the master will configure the third slave and the fourth message the fourth slave, as shown in Figure 10 and Figure 11.

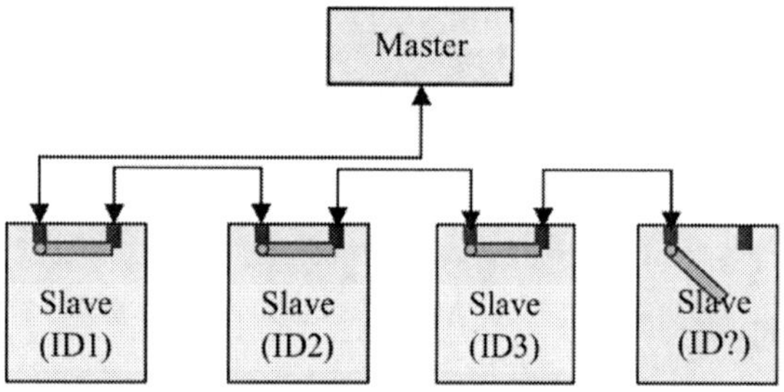

Figure 10. Auto-reconfiguration sequence step 4

So, ultimately, all the devices in the chain will be configured and set to default mode, as shown in Figure 11.

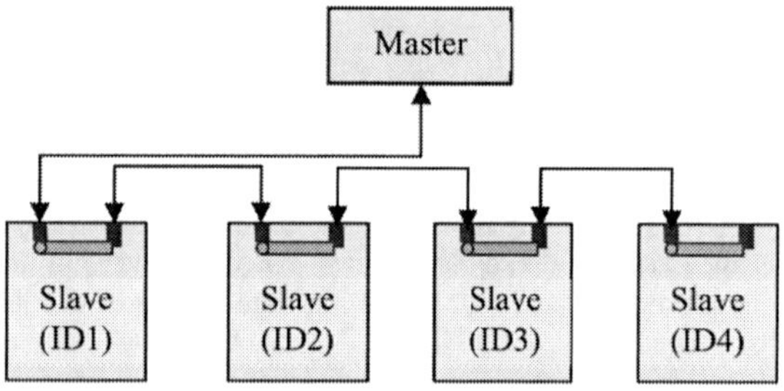

Figure 11. Auto-reconfiguration sequence step 5

Even after the last slave in the chain is configured (as in Figure 11), the master will still be sending configuration messages as before.

However, since all the slaves are in default more and hence no more re-configuration happens, the master will stop to get re-configuration acknowledgement messages back. This will enable the master to deduce that all the slaves in the chain are configured.

IV. SOFTWARE SIMULATION AND RESULTS

A. Simulator architecture

To ensure expected system functionality before development of a hardware prototype, we developed a Modbus slave simulator with added Modbus-A functionality. The Cycle-approximate TLM (Transaction-level modelling) [11] based simulator is capable of simulation of a parametrizable number of slave devices. In the simulation, slave IDs 98 and 99 were reserved for the reconfiguration procedure such that a message (from the master) with the ID 98 will be treated as the reset message that will instruct all the slaves to disconnect their Modbus bridges and to switch into reset mode.

Following that, the master will send messages with ID 99 accompanied with a new slave IDs thereby configuring the recipient slaves.

The same function can be implemented differently with broadcast messages. In Modbus, messages with ID=0 is treated as broadcast messages. Further work will involve use of broadcast messages coupled with function codes depicting reset and config messages.

The autonomous algorithm that enables the master to configure the slave addresses of devices on the network is shown in Figure 12.

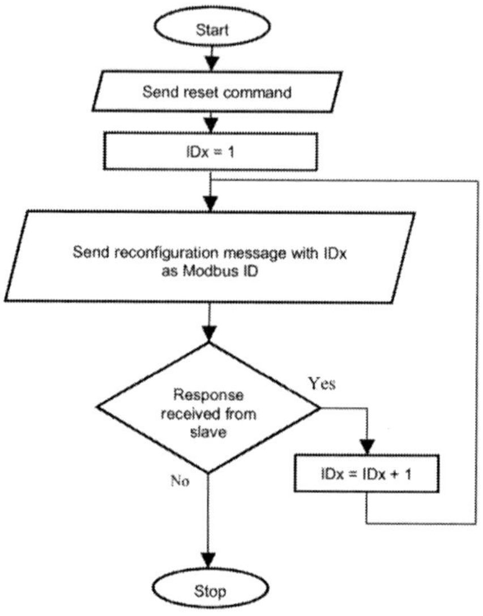

Similarly, the algorithm shown in Figure 13 allows the slaves to get configured autonomously by the master.

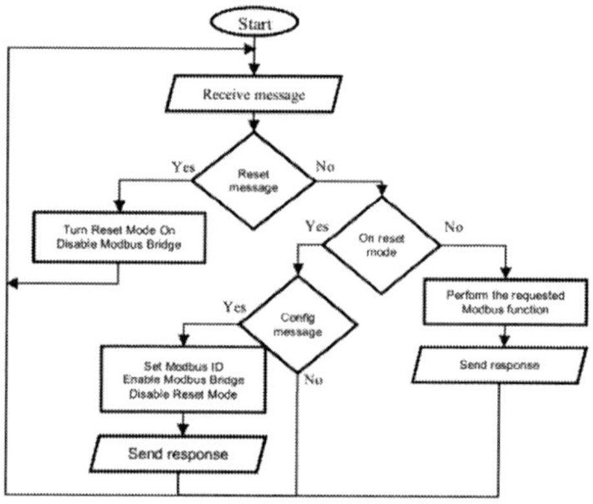

Figure 13. Configuration algorithm on slaves

This enables the slaves to function like any other traditional Modbus slave device under normal working conditions in an infinite loop.

B. Simulation results

Here we present the simulation result of the system with 42 slave devices; from the data captured in the simulator's log. Figure 14 shows the address of the slaves at the start of the simulation. It can be seen that all of the devices have an address of 1; as devices would have out of the box.

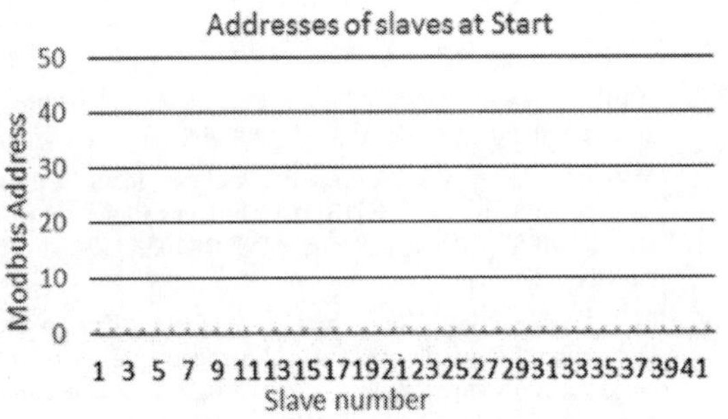

Figure 14. Address of slaves at the start of the simulation

As mentioned in Section III, the Modbus-A master will initally send a reset command which will reset the slave IDs on all the slaves and disconnect its Modbus bridges.

Following that, it will send reset messages to each slave with new slave IDs enabling each slave to set its own ID as per the allocation by the master.

The Modbus addresses of the slaves after the 9th iteration is shown in Figure 15. It can be seen that the first 8 slave devices were give unique IDs from 1 to 8 by the master. It can also be noted that the slaves 9 to 42 do not have IDs as they are in reset mode.

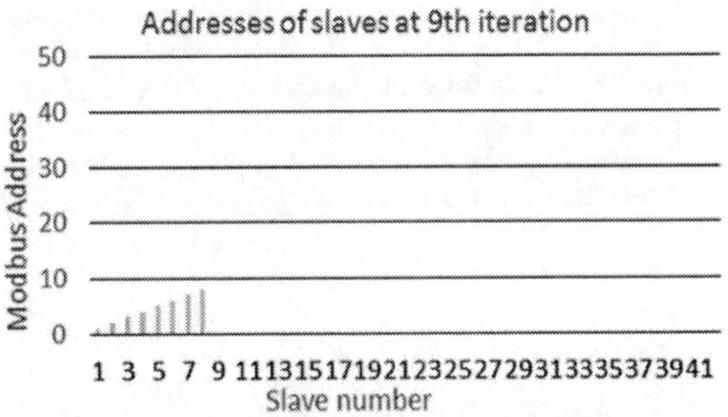

Figure 15. Addresses of slaves after the 9th iteration of the reset logic

Similarly, Figure 16 and Figure 17 show the addresses of the slaves after the 18th and 30th iteration, respectively.

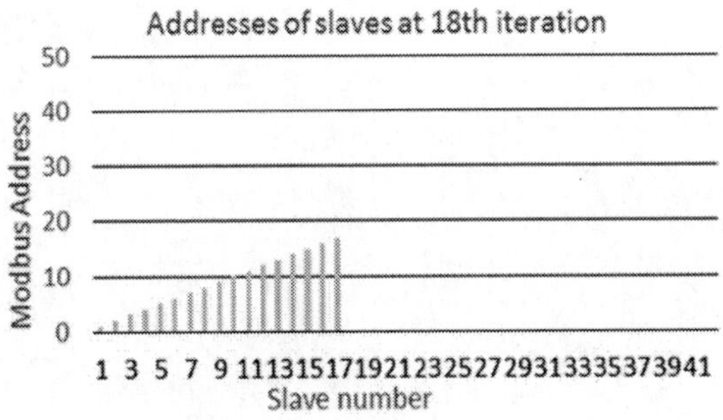

Figure 16. Addresses of slaves after the 18th iteration of the reset logic

It can be seen that 17 of the slaves were reset with unique IDs by the 18th iteration (Figure 16) and 29 of the slaves were reset with unique IDs by the 30th itteration (Figure 17).

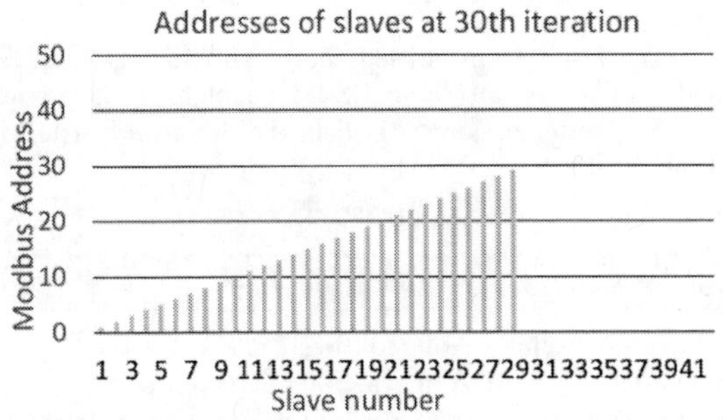

Figure 17. Addresses of slaves after the 30th iteration of the reset logic

Figure 18 shows the address of the slaves after the 44th itteration after the whole reset algorithm was performed. As visible, the master device was able to configure each slave with unique IDs autonomously.

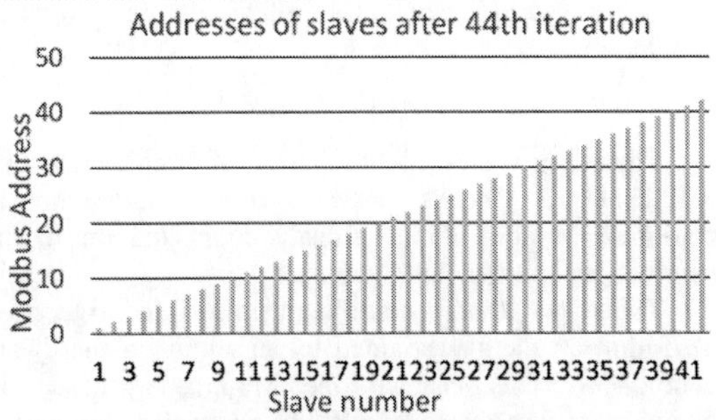

Figure 18. Addresses of slaves after the 44th iteration of the reset logic

V. Hardware Implementation

A RS485 based hardware implementation of a Modbus-A slave is shown in Figure 19.

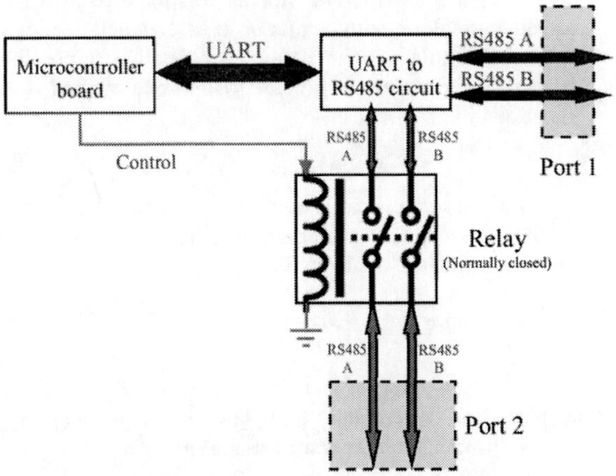

Figure 19. Modbus-A slave implementation

Each Modbus-A slave circuit consisted of a microcontroller board along with a UART (Universal Asynchronous Receiver-Transmitter) to RS485 circuit and a relay. Port 1 is directly connected to the RS485 A and RS485 B connections from the UART to RS485 circuit and the connections to Port 2 are made through the normally closed relay. A control line from the microcontroller board was added to turn the relay on and off as needed.

The test system utilised four such Modbus-A slaves and a PC (with a USB to RS485 adapter) as the master device. The components used in the design are listed in Table I.

TABLE I. COMPONENTS USED

ITEM	MODEL
Microcontroller board	Arduino Mega2560 with 8-bit ATmega2560 microcontroller
Relay	Good Sky GS-SH-205D 5V GS-D Series 1A DPDT Relay
RS485 chip	Maxim MAX3072E

The hardware tests confirmed the functionality of the device as previously established during software simulation.

VI. CONCLUSION

The paper presented Modbus-A, an architecture that will enable a Modbus master device to autonomously configure Modbus slaves already connected on to the common communication medium.

This was made possible using a configuration algorithm on the slaves aided by an additional hardware component. This enabled the Modbus-A master to autonomously reset Modbus IDs of every slave connected using a configuration algorithm. This eliminates the need for individually powering up each Modbus slave and setting its Modbus ID before connecting them into a common communication medium.

The paper explored the implementation aspects of the architecture along with details on tests conducted using a software simulator. The paper also detailed a possible hardware implementation of the system and evaluated its functionality.

ACKNOWLEDGEMENT

This research is partly funded by Innovate UK as part of the Knowledge Transfer Partnership [12] initiative of the government of the United Kingdom.

REFERENCES

[1] Modbus Organization, Inc, "Modbus," 1979. [Online]. Available: http://www.modbus.org/specs.php. [Accessed 19 May 2017].

[2] Modbus Organization, "Modbus application protocol specification v1.1b," 28 December 2006. [Online]. Available: http://www.modbus.org/docs/Modbus_Application_Protocol_V1_1b.pdf. [Accessed 2 June 2017].

[3] R. H. Naismith and D. Areces, "Automatic configuration of network automation devices". USA Patent US 2005/0256939 A1, 17 November 2005.

[4] W. C. Liang, Y. H. Liu, and K. H. Chu, "Method for setting addresses of slave devices in communication network". USA Patent US 9015267B2, 21 April 2015.

[5] IEEE Standard 802.3, "Part3: Carrier sense multiple access with collision detection," 2000 Edition.

[6] Y. P. Grain et al., "Automatic Address Identification Method By Utilizing MODBUS Communication Protocol On RS-485". China Patent CN201410330307.8, 10 February 2016.

[7] C. J. Ching , A. L. Ting, and L. C. Chin, "Design the DNS-Like Smart Switch for Heterogeneous Network Base on SDN Architecture," in *International Computer Symposium (ICS)*, Chiayi, Taiwan, 2016.

[8] C. A. Lloyd, "Automated configuration of device communication settings". USA Patent US 8190697B2, 29 May 2012.

[9] T. Alharbi and M. Portmann, "SProxy ARP - efficient ARP handling in SDN," in *26th International Telecommunication Networks and Applications Conference (ITNAC)*, Dunedin, New Zealand, 2016.

[10] C. Lin, T. Su, and Z. Wang, "Summary of high-availability DHCP service solutions," in *4th IEEE International Conference on Broadband Network and Multimedia Technology (IC-BNMT)*, Shenzhen, China, 2012.

[11] J. R. Harbin and L. S. Indrusiak, "Fast transaction-level dynamic power consumption modelling in priority preemptive wormhole switching networks on chip," in *International Conference on Embedded Computer Systems: Architectures, Modeling, and Simulation (SAMOS XIII)*, Samos, Greece, 2013.

[12] Innovate UK, "Knowledge Transfer Partnerships," Innovate UK, 2017. [Online]. Available: http://ktp.innovateuk.org/. [Accessed 13 June 2017].

Cyber-physical System Control via Industrial Protocol OPC UA

Felix W. Baumann,
Ulrich Odefey, Sebastian Hudert

TWT GmbH Science & Innovation
70565 Stuttgart, Germany
Email: {firstname}.{lastname}@twt-gmbh.de

Michael Falkenthal,
Michael Zimmermann

Institute of Architecture of Application Systems
University of Stuttgart
70569 Stuttgart, Germany
Email: {lastname}@iaas.uni-stuttgart.de

***Abstract*—The integration of cyber-physical systems (CPS) is gaining more and more momentum due to the advent of Industry 4.0. Thereby, one of the main challenges is to facilitate the connection to arbitrary machinery in order to monitor and control these automatically. Such a control flexibilizes production processes by enabling quick adaptions of production steps. Therefore, in this work, a system is described that enables the control of a 3D printer via the industrial standardized Machine-to-Machine (M2M) communication protocol Open Platform Communications Unified Architecture (OPC UA). The system is implemented on the basis of a micro computing platform, in this case a Raspberry Pi 2, and utilises open-source libraries and tools. The implementation creates a cyber-physical system, consisting of a 3D printer, its control system, sensor data acquisition systems and their respective digital representation. With this control system, the usage of consumer-centric 3D printers, such as Fused Deposition Modeling (FDM) printers, in enterprise-like scenarios is enabled. This abstract and universal control mechanism facilitates research in 3D printing control structures and industrial application.**

Keywords*—*Cyber-Physical Systems, 3D Printer, System Control, OPC UA

I. INTRODUCTION

In the industrial domain, especially in current endeavours of Industry 4.0 projects, a common protocol to communicate with machines is the *Open Platform Communications Unified Architecture* (OPC UA) [1]. This protocol allows accessing data from machinery in a read and write manner. It is standardised as International Electrotechnical Commission (IEC) 62541 [1] and, thus, provides a robust basis for sustainable integration scenarios. 3D printers are machines that create physical objects from digital models by a variety of technologies and materials. Thereby, they can be connected and controlled in a number of ways, such as via (i) Universal Serial Bus (USB)-serial cable-bound connection, (ii) WiFi or Ethernet network-bound connection, (iii) a controlling computer, or (iv) manually through interaction at a local control panel. Integrated, abstract and coherent means to control such systems are integral to the application and integration of this technology [2]. OPC UA provides a common way of control and the availability of this abstract interface to this 3D printer facilitates research and industrial application.

3D printers are regarded as CPS because they form a system that matches the physical reality, acquired through sensors, with a digital representation of the 3D printer and the object creation.

In Figure 1, the schematic view of the implementation of the system is depicted. This figure provides the layout and connectivity of the discussed system. The application of this control system within the *SePiA.Pro* project [3], as partially described by Falkenthal et al. [4] and Pfeil et al. [5], is designed to allow for research into process structure analysis and improvement.

The challenges for this integration lie in the diversity of control mechanisms for 3D printers and the fact that most 3D printers are not intended for networked operation natively.

Sensorial data can be integrated into the exposed data on the micro computer and can extend the information provided through this system. The data acquisition is typically performed over I^2C from a digital sensor, similar to systems described by Baumann et al. [6]. This control system can extend a collaborative 3D printing system, such as described by Baumann, Eichhoff, and Roller [7]. Furthermore, it can be utilised to extend or support a common means of communication in distributed 3D printing systems, such as described with the Application Programming Interface (API) for 3D printing by Baumann, Kopp, and Roller [8]. One use-case is the integration of multiple 3D printers in a demonstrator. This demonstrator is used to exemplify scheduling of object creation and is founded on smart service data analytics from 3D printer sensor and additional sensor data. As an example, the 3D print can be paused to allow for manual interaction in case of sensor reading for the temperature sensor in the printhead exceeding a threshold, which can be indicative of jammed filament.

This work describes the connection of existing control mechanisms for 3D printers, a messaging infrastructure for industrial applications and the extension to further data sinks and sources, such as Web Services.

The remainder of this paper is structured as following: In Section I-A, an introduction to the concepts of 3D printing and Additive Manufacturing is provided. Following in Sec-

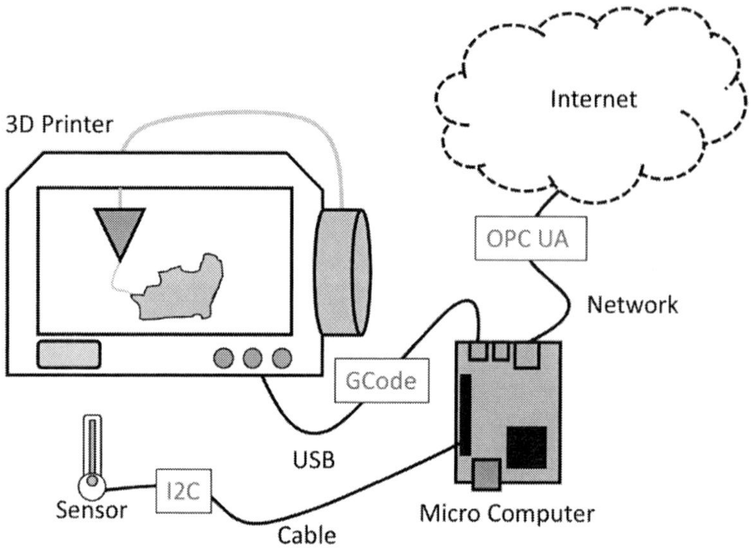

Fig. 1. Schematic View of Implementation

tion I-B, an introduction to the Open Platform Communication Unified Architecture is presented. In Section II, the work is placed within existing research and the objectives are stated. Section III details the required and intended capabilities for the proposed system. The main part of this work is located in Section IV, with details on the architecture and design choices. The paper concludes with a summary in Section V.

A. 3D Printing/Additive Manufacturing

The following short overview on 3D printing is provided for the reader to understand its basics concepts and place this implementation. 3D printing and Additive Manufacturing (AM) are commonly used as synonyms. Both terms describe a variety of technologies to create physical objects from digital models without the requirement for specialised tools, except a 3D printer [9]. The resulting objects can be created from a variety of materials, such as plastics, ceramics, and metals, with commonly only one type of material per resulting object. Different kinds of materials require different kinds of 3D printers and underlying technologies. The objects are commonly created by a directed, layer-wise stacking, curing or extrusion of a material [10], [11]. The 3D printing process and the corresponding results can be influenced by a number of environmental and inherent factors, such as vibration, temperature or quality of material. To assess and possibly counteract these influences, sensors are employed to acquire data from the 3D printing process.

B. Open Platform Communications Unified Architecture

Open Platform Communications Unified Architecture (OPC UA) is a platform-independent standard for machine-to-machine (M2M) communication, e.g., between clients and servers on various types of networks [12]. It is intended to facilitate information exchange between machines. Thereby, OPC UA is an extension of the older OPC standards and adds, among others, the ability to semantically describe the transmitted machine data. Due to its fundamental design on the basis of a service oriented architecture [13], OPC UA has been adopted in a number of domains such as industrial machinery, power grids, home or building automation, and smart devices [14]. This way, it facilitates the interoperability of the involved systems and evolves as a multi-standard platform, which it initially was intended and specified for by the OPC Foundation.

II. Related Work

For an overview of existing control mechanisms and architectures for the remote control of AM machinery, we refer to Baumann, Kopp and Roller [15], where a detailed discussion of related work is presented. Concepts such as Cloud Based Manufacturing, Hardware and Manufacturing as a Service are also provided in the overview by Baumann and Roller [16]. In the work by Berteslmeier, Schöne and Trächtle [17], the authors presented a similar control system using OPC UA with focus on intelligent products. Existing control mechanisms for 3D printers lack the ability to incorporate physical feedback from the machine and lacks extensibility. In this paper, we provide a control mechanism for 3D printers that is based on an established industrial communication protocol, thus enabling the integration of AM machinery into existing software and control ecosystems. This integration requires the presence of a micro computing platform that facilitates networking and translation services to machines that were previously not networked but connected directly to control systems via USB. The utilization of an existing protocol reduces the implementation efforts and enables a low-cost solution for remote access, management and control of these machines. Due to flexibility in the design of the approach, other machines and sensors can be integrated and controlled or used as data sources. With this added control capability, 3D printers can be integrated into smart environments and production systems.

III. Capabilities of the Control System

The following capabilities are already implemented within the control system running on the micro computer, as illustrated in Figure 1. The capabilities are specifically justified to cover the basic requirements of operation of a 3D printer.

- Direct control of printhead: The movement of the printhead can be controlled by defining movement accuracy, movement speed, as well as x, y, z coordinates.
- Control and monitoring of temperatures and other printer inherent sensors: Current printbed and tool temperatures as well as their historical data can be obtained.
- Upload of files to 3D printer: Files containing the model to print can be uploaded and stored to the 3D printer's SDCard or to the micro controller, depending on the user's needs.
- Control of 3D printer operation: General commands to control the operation mode of the 3D printer, such as start, pause and stop operations, can be triggered.
- Status control and monitoring of 3D printer: Inherent 3D printer status information and external sensor data acquisition is implemented and can be obtained.
- File availability information: To manage already uploaded files, the data structure of the control system and the 3D printer's SDCard can be retrieved.

These features are implemented in the system and described in the following Section IV.

IV. Implementation Basis

The system is implemented utilising the *node-opcua* library [18], available for *NodeJS* [19]. This library provides both server and client bindings for *JavaScript*. The server component, which exposes the *OPC UA* data from the 3D printer and the system to the client, consists of a *JavaScript* file that implements the required functionality. The system exposes internal properties, such as Central Processing Unit (CPU) temperature, CPU utilisation, memory availability, as historical data nodes, thus, enabling clients to subscribe to data change events for this data. Historical data nodes denote objects that carry and present historical information of their previous states or readings. Furthermore, external or 3D printer inherent data, such as bed and tool temperature, are exposed as historical data nodes. The sensor data acquisition is performed directly from the *JavaScript* server program, utilising Inter-Integrated Circui (I^2C) communication, provided via the *i2c-bus NodeJS* library [20].

The acquisition of data from and control of the 3D printer are performed by using the *OctoPrint* [21] software. This software is available for the Linux platform and suitable for deployment on micro computers, such as a *Raspberry Pi 2* [22]. The software provides control mechanism for a large number of different 3D printers, mostly over a USB serial

Fig. 2. 3D Printer

connection. The micro computer provides the capabilities to interface with the 3D printer via the network, as the 3D printer itself does not necessarily provide a networking interface.

The control of a printer is implemented following the GCode protocol [23], which is a line based control format. GCode is a numerical control programming language standardised as ISO 6983 [23], however, variations in the implementation by the manufacturers exist. For this experiment, a *Tevo Tarantula* [24] 3D printer (see Figure 2) is flashed with the *Marlin* [25] firmware to be used with the *OctoPrint* software. *OctoPrint* exposes all its functionality over a Hypertext Transfer Protocol (HTTP) Representational State Transfer (RESTful) API. This API is utilised to communicate and control the 3D printer via local API calls from the server component. Authorisation in *OctoPrint* is disabled as only local communication is allowed.

The communication flow of the client, the implemented server and the 3D printer are depicted in Figure 3. This figure shows that the polling of status from the 3D printer and its subsequent processing and dispatch to the user is performed in a loop while the issued command is performed. The *OctoPrint* software does not support Websocket technology for continuous connection to its API. As an example, the command to print a specific file from the SDCard is discussed in the following.

When the user or client issues this command, the system checks with the 3D printer and then actually issues the command on the 3D printer. Thereby, the system must check for connectivity, availability of the SDCard, and the correct status, i.e., no-error, print-ready state. For asynchronous communication over the API, the *request* library [26] in conjunction with the *form-data* [27] library are used.

To provide, direct and synchronous communication to the user, most communication with the API is performed synchronously, using the *sync-request* library [28], which blocks the execution of the server while waiting for the communi-

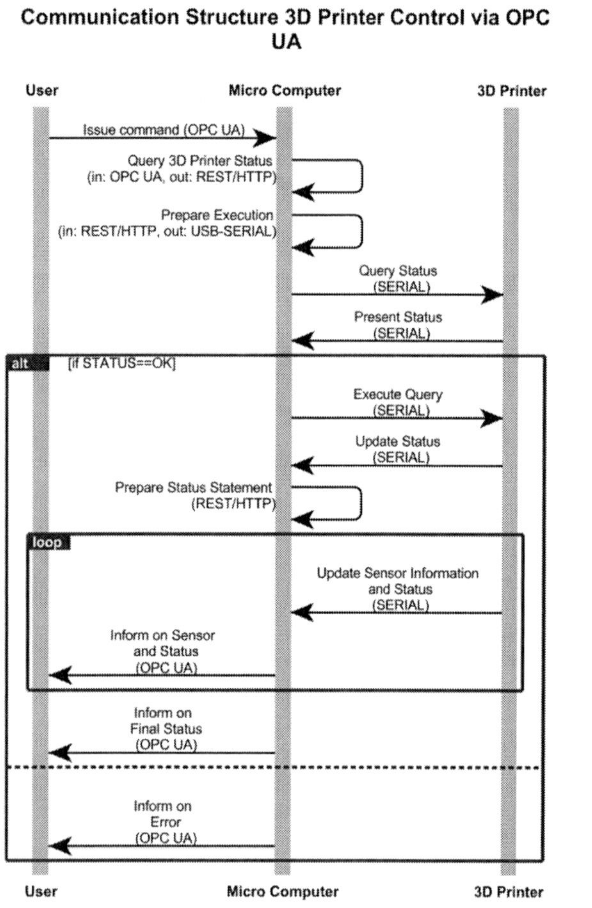

Fig. 3. Communication Structure between User, Client, and 3D Printer

cation results and, thus, is unsuitable for scalable application deployment. The processing of the status information of the printer, such as print completion rate, 3D printer status, and temperatures is performed by a pull-mechanism that is triggered by the server.

Figure 4 displays the stacking structure of the components within the system. The basis is the micro computing system, or single board computer, on which a Linux operating system is running. The individual *NodeJS* libraries are displayed at the topmost layer.

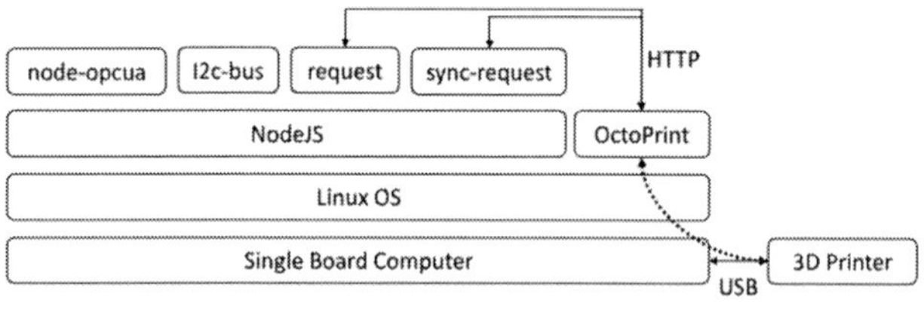

Fig. 4. System Structure

Push notification is possible with *OctoPrint*, but limited to two messages per second. The interfacing of a client with the implemented server is shown as a screenshot in Figure 5. In this figure, three subscribed data nodes and the expanded tree structure of the nodes are visible.

The implementation is available as a file-system image upon request from the authors, pre-configured for use on a *Raspberry Pi 2* system and a *Marlin* firmware based 3D printer, as listed as supported on the *OctoPrint* website.

V. CONCLUSION

This paper describes the design of the implementation of a control system for a CPS, a 3D printer and its associated sensors. This system is based on the widely used standard *OPC UA* for industrial M2M communication. Through the exposure of sensor and machine data via *OPC UA* the implementation in industrial settings is facilitated. The system developed facilitates the complete control of a variety of 3D printers using *OPC UA*. It was shown how the control of such a system is enabled by transformation of one common protocol to another common protocol by open-source software. The software is implemented with the described capabilities and the potential for extension in future iterations. Future iterations of this software are planned to allow control and communication over other protocols, such as *MQTT* [29] and *Woopsa* [30]. Furthermore, data source integration using asynchronous connections, such as Websockets are to be integrated.

Acknowledgments

This work is partially funded by the project SePiA.Pro (01MD16013F) of the BMWi program Smart Service World.

REFERENCES

[1] TC 65/SC 65E, "IEC 62541-100:2015 OPC Unified Architecture - Part 100: Device Interface," International Standard, International Electrotechnical Commission, IEC 62541-100, 3 2015. [Online]. Available: https://webstore.iec.ch/publication/21987

[2] Y. Lu, K. C. Morris, and S. P. Frechette, "Current Standards Landscape for Smart Manufacturing Systems," National Institute for Standards and Technology (NIST), NISTIR 8107, 2016. [Online]. Available: https://dx.doi.org/10.6028/NIST.IR.8107

[3] Deutsches Forschungszentrum für Künstliche Intelligenz *et al.*, "SePiA.Pro – Service platform for the intelligent optimization of prodcution lines," retrieved Nov., 2017. [Online]. Available: http://projekt-sepiapro.de

[4] M. Falkenthal *et al.*, "Requirements for policies in industrial data sharing scenarios," in *Proceedings of the 11th Symposium and Summer School On Service-Oriented Computing*, 2017, in Press.

[5] M. Pfeil *et al.*, "Smart services - the smart implementation of Industry 4.0," in *NAFEMS Seminar Simulation von Composites – Bereit für Industrie 4.0?*, 10 2016. [Online]. Available: https://www.researchgate.net/publication/317687064_Smart_services_-_the_smart_implementation_of_Industry_40

[6] F. W. Baumann *et al.*, "Sensors on 3D Printers for Cloud Printing Service," in *Proceedings of the 2016 International Conference on Sustainable Energy, Environment and Information Engineering*. DEStech Publications, Inc., 3 2016, pp. 571–577. [Online]. Available: http://dx.doi.org/10.12783/dteees/seeie2016/4689

[7] F. W. Baumann, J. Eichhoff, and D. Roller, *Collaborative Cloud Printing Service*. Springer International Publishing, 2016, pp. 77–85. [Online]. Available: http://dx.doi.org/10.1007/978-3-319-46771-9_10

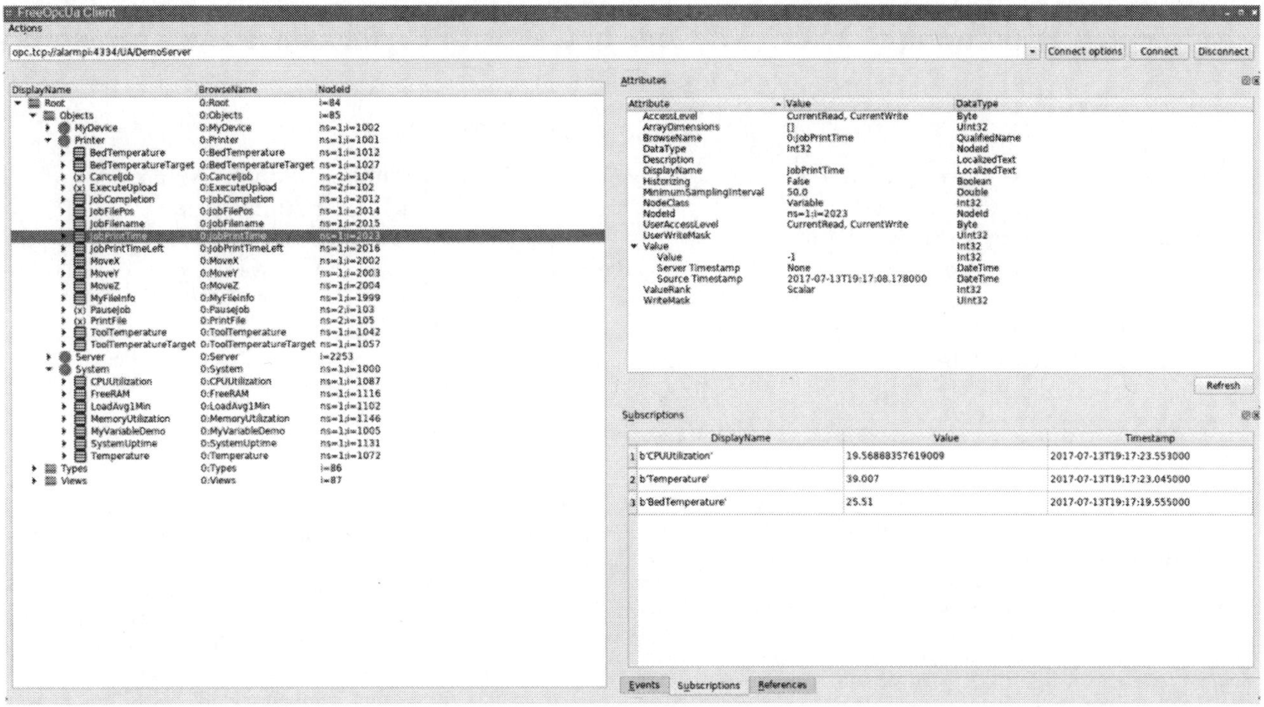

Fig. 5. Screenshot of OPC UA Client

[8] F. W. Baumann, O. Kopp, and D. Roller, "Universal API for 3D Printers," in *INFORMATIK 2016. Lecture Notes in Informatics (LNI)*, H. C. Mayr and M. Pinzger, Eds., vol. P-259. Gesellschaft für Informatik, 2016, pp. 1611–1622. [Online]. Available: http://subs.emis.de/LNI/Proceedings/Proceedings259/article155.html

[9] I. Gibson, D. W. Rosen, and B. Stucker, *Additive Manufacturing Technologies: Rapid Prototyping to Direct Digital Manufacturing*, 1st ed. Springer Publishing Company, Incorporated, 2009.

[10] N. Guo and M. C. Leu, "Additive manufacturing: technology, applications and research needs," *Frontiers of Mechanical Engineering*, vol. 8, no. 3, pp. 215–243, 2013. [Online]. Available: http://dx.doi.org/10.1007/s11465-013-0248-8

[11] P. Kulkarni, A. Marsan, and D. Dutta, "A review of process planning techniques in layered manufacturing," *Rapid Prototyping Journal*, vol. 6, no. 1, pp. 18–35, 2000. [Online]. Available: https://doi.org/10.1108/13552540010309859

[12] F. Palm *et al.*, "open62541 - der offene OPC UA Stack," in *Jahreskolloquium "Kommunikation in der Automation" (KommA)*, 2014, pp. 1–9. [Online]. Available: http://publica.fraunhofer.de/dokumente/N-322220.html

[13] S.-H. Leitner and W. Mahnke, "OPC UA - Service-oriented Architecture for Industrial Applications," *Softwaretechnik-Trends*, vol. 26, 2006.

[14] T. Hadlich, "Providing device integration with opc ua," in *2006 4th IEEE International Conference on Industrial Informatics*, 10 2006, pp. 263–268.

[15] F. W. Baumann, O. Kopp, and D. Roller, "Abstract API for 3D Printing Hardware and Software Resources," *International Journal of Advanced Manufacturing Technology*, pp. 1–17, 2016.

[16] F. W. Baumann and D. Roller, "3D Printing Process Pipeline on the Internet," in *Proceedings of the 8th Central European Workshop on Services and their Composition (ZEUS 2016)*, 2016, pp. 29–36. [Online]. Available: http://ceur-ws.org/Vol-1562/paper4.pdf

[17] F. Bertelsmeier, S. Schöne, and A. Trächtler, "Development and design of intelligent product carriers for flexible networked control of distributed manufacturing processes," in *2016 24th Mediterranean Conference on Control and Automation (MED)*, 6 2016, pp. 755–760.

[18] E. Rossignon, "Build OPC UA applications in JavaScript and NodeJS," retrieved Nov., 2017. [Online]. Available: http://node-opcua.github.io

[19] Node.js Foundation, "Node.js," retrieved Nov., 2017. [Online]. Available: https://nodejs.org

[20] B. Cooke, "i2c-bus," retrieved Nov., 2017. [Online]. Available: https://www.npmjs.com/package/i2c-bus

[21] G. Häußge, "Octoprint - the snappy web interface for your 3d printer," retrieved Nov., 2017. [Online]. Available: http://octoprint.org

[22] Raspberry Pi Foundation, "Raspberry Pi - Teach, Learn, and Make with Raspberry Pi," retrieved Nov., 2017. [Online]. Available: https://www.raspberrypi.org

[23] ISO/TC 184/SC 1 Physical device control, "ISO 6983-1:2009 Automation systems and integration – Numerical control of machines – Program format and definitions of address words – Part 1: Data format for positioning, line motion and contouring control systems," International Standard, International Organization for Standardization, ISO 6983-1, 12 2009. [Online]. Available: https://www.iso.org/standard/34608.html

[24] J. Choo, "Marlin Firmware for Tevo Tarantula 3d Printer," retrieved Nov., 2017. [Online]. Available: https://github.com/josephchoo/TevoTarantulaMarlin

[25] Marlin dev team, "Optimized firmware for RepRap 3D printers based on the Arduino platform," retrieved Nov., 2017. [Online]. Available: https://github.com/MarlinFirmware/Marlin

[26] M. Rogers *et al.*, "request," retrieved Nov., 2017. [Online]. Available: https://www.npmjs.com/package/request

[27] A. Indigo *et al.*, "form-data," retrieved Nov., 2017. [Online]. Available: https://github.com/form-data/form-data

[28] F. Lindesay, "sync-request," retrieved Nov., 2017. [Online]. Available: https://www.npmjs.com/package/sync-request

[29] R. J. Cohn *et al.*, "MQTT Version 3.1.1," retrieved Nov., 2017. [Online]. Available: http://docs.oasis-open.org/mqtt/mqtt/v3.1.1/os/mqtt-v3.1.1-os.html

[30] F. Birling, F. Segginger, and F. Chevalley, "Web Object Oriented Protocol for Software and Automation," retrieved Nov., 2017. [Online]. Available: http://www.woopsa.org

Automated Translation of MATLAB Code to C++ with Performance and Traceability

Geir Yngve Paulsen
and Stuart Clark
Simula Research Laboratory, Norway
Email: geirpa@gmail.com, stuart@simula.no

Bjørn Nordmoen, Sergey Nenakhov
and Aron Andersson
WesternGeco, Norway
Email: {nordmoen, snenakhov, AAnderson11}@slb.com

Xing Cai
Simula Research Laboratory, Norway
University of Oslo, Norway
Email: xingca@simula.no

Hans Petter Dahle
Fornebu Consulting, Norway
Email: Hans.Petter.Dahle@fornebuconsulting.com

***Abstract*—In this paper, we discuss the implementation and performance of *m2cpp*: an automated translator from MATLAB code to its matching Armadillo counterpart in the C++ language. A non-invasive strategy has been adopted, meaning that the user of *m2cpp* does not insert annotations or additional code lines into the input serial MATLAB code. Instead, a combination of code analysis, automated preprocessing and a user-editable metainfo file ensures that *m2cpp* overcomes some specialties of the MATLAB language, such as implicit typing of variables and multiple return values from functions. Thread-based parallelisation, using either OpenMP or Intel's Threading Building Blocks (TBB) library, can also be carried out by *m2cpp* for designated for-loops. Such an automated and non-invasive strategy allows maintaining an independent MATLAB code base that is favoured by algorithm developers, while an updated translation into the easily readable C++ counterpart can be obtained at any time. Illustrating examples from seismic data processing are provided in this paper, with performance results obtained on multicore Sandy Bridge CPUs and Intel's Knights-Landing Xeon Phi processor.**

Keywords*–*Code translation; Seismology; Image processing; MATLAB; C++.

I. Introduction

MATLAB® is a popular software for computational mathematics, particularly because of its accessibility for scientists and engineers as a high-level scripting language. This ease of use and a large library of toolboxes make MATLAB a good choice for testing and prototyping new algorithms. However, once the algorithms are tested, the ability to sufficiently optimise MATLAB code may become a key concern. MATLAB is a scripting language, so it cannot make use of compile-time based optimisations, such as latency-grouped instructions. While MATLAB offers multi-process based parallelisation, multi-thread optimisation can in many cases work better on current high-performance systems [1]. As a result of these issues, in situations for which optimisation is extremely important, rewriting the MATLAB code in another language, such as C++, could be a remedy. For that purpose, the Armadillo C++ library was developed to enable MATLAB-like syntax in a C++ setting [2][3].

Although Armadillo has adopted a MATLAB-resembling syntax for matrix and vector based computations, there are still distinctive syntax differences between Armadillo and MATLAB. For example, Armadillo's indexing of matrix and vector entries starts from 0, whereas indices in MATLAB start from 1. Another example is extracting columns or rows from a matrix, which has a drastically different syntax in MATLAB than in Armadillo. (An incomplete list of the syntax differences can be found in [3].) Manually translating a MATLAB code to its C++ counterpart in Armadillo is thus tedious and potentially error prone. Since there is an almost one-to-one mapping between the two high-level syntaxes, automated MATLAB-to-Armadillo translation is theoretically possible. However, MATLAB and C++ are two fundamentally different languages. Some inherent language features of MATLAB pose challenges to an automated code translator. Two such examples are implicit typing of variables and multiple return values from functions. To handle these challenges, some existing MATLAB translators ask the user to insert annotations of variable declaration and initialisation. Such an invasive approach is not very user-friendly, and may also cause problems if algorithm developers want to further change the MATLAB code.

Therefore, we aim for an automated MATLAB-to-C++ translator that adopts a non-invasive strategy. This is achieved by combining (1) code analysis enabled inside the translator, (2) a fully automated preprocessor that identifies the actual types of all variables used in a MATLAB program, and (3) an accompanying metainfo file that allows user editing and, if necessary, introduction of special translation rules designated for some of the MATLAB code lines. At the same time, we certainly do not want the auto-translated C++ code to lose the capability of parallel computing, which is already available through MATLAB's Parallel Computing Toolbox and Distributed Computing Server [4]. We have focused on parallelising designated for-loops (through MATLAB's `parfor` construct) as one inherent step of the auto-translation, making use of either OpenMP [5] or Intel's Threading Building Blocks (TBB) [6] library in a shared-memory setting.

This paper thus presents the design and implementation of *m2cpp*, an automated MATLAB-to-Armadillo translator. It has been substantially enhanced from its initial version (named *Matlab2cpp* [7]). Using illustrating examples from seismic data processing, we will show the capability of *m2cpp*. Performance of the auto-translated C++ programs is measured for both serial and parallel executions, compared with the original MATLAB versions. The tested hardware platforms involve multicore Xeon Sandy Bridge CPUs and Intel's second-generation Xeon Phi processor (Knights Landing). As a benefit of the readable C++ code, which retains the same structure and variable names of the original MATLAB code, we also demonstrate a particular example of further performance optimisation of the auto-generated C++ code.

The remainder of the paper is organised as follows. Section II summarises the overall design and main features of the *m2cpp* translator. Section III uses four real-world examples to compare the performance of MATLAB, auto-translated and manually optimised C++ codes, in both serial and parallel settings. Section IV places the present paper in the landscape of existing relevant work, whereas Section V provides a few concluding remarks and some thoughts on future work.

II. Design and Implementation

A. Overall Structure

As mentioned above, the aim of *m2cpp* is to facilitate an automatic and non-invasive translation from MATLAB code to the matching Armadillo counterpart in the C++ language. The non-invasiveness refers to that the user of *m2cpp* does not need to insert any annotation or extra coding into a serial MATLAB program before passing it to the translator. The *m2cpp* translator itself is written in the Python language, with a tailor made top-down recursive descent parser [8] that follows the same approach adopted by ANTLR [9]. The parser reads the input MATLAB code and internally sets up an abstract syntax tree, which is then subjected to a post-order tree walk [8] for necessary code analysis and translation to the resulting C++ code. Tasks of code analysis include, e.g., identifying MATLAB functions that return multiple values, which are translated as additional input arguments of the corresponding C++ functions. Another important task of code analysis is in connection with thread-based parallelisation of for-loops, where some variables have to be made private per thread to avoid race conditions.

B. Metainfo File

For the automatic translation of a MATLAB program to work correctly, *m2cpp* also relies on an accompanying metainfo file, which has the same name as the (principal) MATLAB input file but ending with `*.m.py`. This approach ensures that the *m2cpp* translator is non-invasive to the input MATLAB code, because the additional information needed for the code translation is provided in a separate file, easily editable by the user if needed. The metainfo file consists of three parts, where the first part is a list of all variables to be encountered, containing the name and type of each variable. This part of information can be automatically filled out by an automated preprocessor (see below). The second part of the metainfo file, marked as the *includes segment*, contains explicit C++ `include` statements needed by the Armadillo library, as well as necessary `include` statements when the entire source code is spread over several files. These `include` statements are figured out by the automated preprocessor and will later be inserted into the translated C++ code. The third part of the metainfo file, marked as the *verbatims segment*, is optional. Here, the user has the possibility of introducing special translation rules. That is, the user can dictate how a specific code line in the MATLAB program should be translated into C++, without following the general translation rules of *m2cpp*.

C. Preprocessing

There is a preprocessing functionality with *m2cpp*. The main purpose is to automatically prepare the metainfo file with respect to identifying the actual type of each variable, which is needed for the subsequent MATLAB-to-Armadillo translation. Automatic identification of variable types is achieved by autonomously running a copy of the MATLAB program with inserted `dump` function calls for recording all the state information, including the actual data type of all encountered MATLAB variables. The recorded data type information is then automatically extracted and inserted into the metainfo file. Even if *m2cpp* is used on a computer without a MATLAB installation, the preprocessor of *m2cpp* will automatically identify all the encountered MATLAB variables, while providing a reasonable guess of the variable types. The user can then make corrections to the variable type information in the metainfo file, if necessary.

In a typical code development scenario, where the input MATLAB code is repeatedly changed, an existing metainfo file can be reused provided that the changes on the MATLAB side do not introduce new variables or non-standard statements that require a special translation rule. Even if such changes take place on the MATLAB side, it is often more convenient for the user to directly edit the metainfo file, without having to re-run the preprocessor of *m2cpp*.

D. Parallelisation of For-Loops

The focus of *m2cpp* with respect to parallelisation is on MATLAB for-loops that have independent iterations. These for-loops are assumed to be already marked as `parfor` constructs in the MATLAB program. The *m2cpp* translator considers shared memory and adopts thread-based parallelisation of the designated MATLAB for-loops. More specifically, the user of *m2cpp* can freely choose between parallelisation enabled by the OpenMP [5] standard or Intel's TBB library [6]. For the case of OpenMP, a compiler directive `#pragma omp parallel for` is automatically inserted before each designated for-loop. For the case of TBB, the code lines shown in Figure 1, making use of C++11's lambda expressions, are automatically inserted for each designated for-loop.

```
tbb::parallel_for(
  tbb::blocked_range<size_t>(1,num_points+1),
    [&](const tbb::blocked_range<size_t>& _range) {
      // declaration of thread-private variables ...
      for(size_t i=_range.begin();i!=_range.end();++i)
      {
        // loop iteration body ...
      }
    }
);
```

Figure 1. An example of parallelising a for-loop in TBB.

Common for both parallelisation approaches, *m2cpp* is able to properly introduce temporary variables that are private to each thread, so that race conditions will not happen.

E. Limitations

It should be noted that *m2cpp* is not supposed to translate any MATLAB code. The automated translation of *m2cpp* is restricted to MATLAB programs that make use of matrix and vector computations that are covered by the functionality of the Armadillo library. Nevertheless, we have included a couple of new C++ functions beyond the original functionality of Armadillo, so that typical plotting functions of MATLAB can also be automatically translated by *m2cpp*.

In addition, two special features of the MATLAB language can not be handled by *m2cpp*. First, MATLAB allows a variable to implicitly change its type within a program. This is fundamentally in contrast to the static typing rule of C++. Although for some cases, it is possible to introduce a new variable (having a different name) in the C++ code to resolve the implicit change of a MATLAB variable type, we have decided to not support this, due to the infrequent occurrence of variable type changes in MATLAB programs. The other special MATLAB feature is dynamic expansion of matrices and vectors. It typically happens with variables that are declared with empty storage but are dynamically expanded inside a loop. In principle, a detailed code analysis can deduce the final size of dynamically expanded matrices or vectors, so that the translated C++ code can declare the matrices or vectors with a correct size. But this requires a rather elaborate code analyser, not yet supported in *m2cpp*. Another cumbersome and inefficient option is to frequently insert a call to the `resize` function of Armadillo, which we deem non-viable. As a remedy, though, the user can introduce a special translation rule in the metainfo file to prescribe a correct size for each dynamically-expanded MATLAB matrix or vector variable.

III. Results

A. SeismicLab

We have chosen the open-source MATLAB package SeismicLab [10], which concerns seismic data processing, for verifying the correctness of *m2cpp*-translated C++ code. Moreover, we want to measure the speed of the translated C++ code, in both serial and parallel computing settings, for a comparison with the original MATLAB code.

For this paper, four relatively computation-heavy demo programs from SeismicLab have been chosen. They are `parabolic_moveout_demo`, `radon_demo_1`, `moveout_demo` and `fx_decon_demo`. (Each demo program spans several `*.m` files.) We have enlarged the computation size for all the four demos by increasing the resolution of the original input data files with help of linear interpolation. For the first two demos, which share the same input data file, the new computation size is 4004×1568, whereas the new computation size is 4176×2432 and 2004×1600 for the last two demos, respectively.

The numerical results produced by the auto-translated C++ codes have been carefully compared with those from the original MATLAB codes, to ensure the correctness of the code translation done by *m2cpp*. In the remainder of this section, our focus is thus directed to the serial and parallel efficiency of the auto-translated C++ codes.

B. Example of Parabolic Moveout

Readability of the auto-translated C++ code is ensured by retaining the exact same coding structure and variable names as in the original MATLAB code. For instance, let us first show in Figure 2 the main computation segment from the original MATLAB code for the example of parabolic moveout.

```
for it = 1:ntau
  for iq = 1:nq
    time =  tau(it) + q(iq)*(h/hmax).^2 ;
    s = zeros(2*L+1,nh);

    for ig = -L:L;
      ts = time + (ig-1)*dt;

      for ih = 1:nh
        is = ts(ih)/dt+1;
        i1 = floor(is);
        i2 = i1 + 1;

        if i1>=1 & i2<=nt ;
          a = is-i1;
          s(ig+L+1,ih) = (1.-a)*d(i1,ih) + a*d(i2,ih);
        end;
      end
    end

    s = s.*H;
    s1  = sum( (sum(s,2)).^2);
    s2  = sum( sum(s.^2));
    S(it,iq) = s1-s2;
  end
end
```

Figure 2. The original MATLAB code of the computational core of the parabolic moveout example.

The MATLAB code segment shown in Figure 2 constitutes the computational core of the parabolic moveout example. It is in fact a nested for-loop of four layers. The corresponding code segment of the auto-translated C++ code is shown in Figure 3. We can see that the C++ code adopts the Armadillo syntax while maintaining the same readability as the original MATLAB code. (We remark that the `%` operator in Armadillo does element-wise multiplication.)

```
for (it=1; it<=ntau; it++) {
  for (iq=1; iq<=nq; iq++) {
    time = tau(it-1)+q(iq-1)*arma::square(h/hmax) ;
    s = arma::zeros<mat>(2*L+1, nh) ;

    for (ig=-(L); ig<=L; ig++) {
      ts = time+(ig-1)*dt ;
      for (ih=1; ih<=nh; ih++) {
        is = ts(ih-1)/dt+1 ;
        i1 = std::floor(is) ;
        i2 = i1+1 ;

        if (i1>=1&&i2<=nt) {
          a = is-i1 ;
          s(ig+L, ih-1) = (1.-a)*d(i1-1, ih-1)
                          +a*d(i2-1, ih-1) ;
        }
      }
    }
    s = s%H ;
    s1 = arma::as_scalar(
           arma::sum(arma::square(arma::sum(s, 1)))) ;
    s2 = arma::sum(arma::sum(arma::square(s))) ;
    S(it-1, iq-1) = s1-s2 ;
  }
}
```

Figure 3. The auto-translated C++ code of the computational core of the parabolic moveout example.

Auto-parallelisation of the outermost `it`-indexed for-loop can also be carried out by *m2cpp*, via either OpenMP or TBB as described in Section II-D. This merely requires adding a comment of form `%#PARFOR` above the target for-loop in the MATLAB input code. (The auto-parallelised C++ code is not shown.)

C. Time Measurements

To study the performance of the auto-translated C++ codes, we used two representative hardware platforms: a dual-socket 2×8-core Sandy Bridge server and a 68-core Knights-Landing (KNL) Xeon Phi processor. The hardware specification can be found in Table I. The compilation flags used for the C++ codes were `-Ofast`, `-xHost`, `-D NDEBUG`, `-D ARMA_NO_DEBUG`, `-lmkl_intel_lp64`, `-lmkl_core`, `-lmkl_sequential`. It should be noticed that Intel's Math Kernel Library (MKL) is invoked by the auto-generated C++ codes when applicable. This is fair with respect to the original MATLAB codes, which also internally invoke Intel's MKL when applicable. For the codes parallelised with TBB, the additional compilation flags `-std=c++11` and `-ltbb` were also used. Each time measurement listed in Tables II-V was obtained by running the code at least three times and reporting the fastest time.

TABLE I. HARDWARE SPECIFICATION OF THE TWO TESTBED PLATFORMS USED.

Platform	Sandy Bridge server	KNL
Processor model	E5-2670 (dual socket)	Xeon Phi 7250
Clock frequency	2.6 GHz	1.4 GHz
Core count	16 (2 × 8)	68
Compiler	icpc v17.0.1	icpc v17.0.0

Table II compares the serial performance of the auto-translated C++ code, i.e., executed on only one hardware core of each machine. Since MATLAB (version R2016a) is only available on the dual-socket server, time measurements of the original MATLAB code are thus only reported for that system. It is clear that the *m2cpp*-translated C++ versions run considerably faster than the MATLAB counterparts on the dual-socket server. (The only exception is the `fx_decon` example, for which the core computation is done using Intel's MKL for both MATLAB and C++ versions.) Moreover, the single-core C++ performance obtained on KNL is lower than that obtained on a single core of the Sandy Bridge CPU, because of a much lower clock frequency and the absence of an L3 cache.

TABLE II. SINGLE-CORE TIME USAGE (IN SECONDS) OF FOUR DEMO PROGRAMS FROM THE SEISMICLAB PACKAGE.

Code	MATLAB	C++	C++
Platform	Server	Server	KNL
Parabolic_moveout	261.7	59.5	133.2
Radon1	33.6	19.0	41.6
Moveout	3.0	0.9	1.6
Fx_decon	2.7	2.0	4.0

Regarding the parallel performance, Tables III-IV show that the auto-translated C++ programs (using either OpenMP or TBB) get speedup when the number of threads increases up to the same number as physical cores. It should be remarked that MATLAB's `parfor` only works for the `fx_decon` example, due to a rather conservative MATLAB runtime system, although the iterations are actually independent in the other three examples. Therefore, parallel MATLAB performance is only reported for the `fx_decon` example in Table IV, not the other three examples in Table III.

TABLE III. PARALLEL TIME USAGE (IN SECONDS) OF SEISMICLAB'S `PARABOLIC_MOVEOUT`, `RADON1` AND `MOVEOUT` DEMOS.

Parabolic_moveout				
	Dual-socket server		KNL	
# threads	OpenMP	TBB	OpenMP	TBB
1	59.3	59.9	126.4	128.5
2	30.1	30.0	84.6	66.1
4	15.5	15.3	44.2	32.9
8	8.1	7.9	22.1	17.8
16	4.4	4.4	11.4	9.4
32	4.7	4.2	6.1	5.0
68			3.0	3.6
Radon1				
	Dual-socket server		KNL	
# threads	OpenMP	TBB	OpenMP	TBB
1	18.4	19.1	41.1	42.0
2	10.8	10.6	22.9	24.0
4	6.5	6.4	13.6	13.8
8	4.4	4.4	8.3	8.8
16	4.0	3.5	5.6	6.5
32	3.8	3.6	4.3	4.9
68			3.8	4.5
Moveout				
	Dual-socket server		KNL	
# threads	OpenMP	TBB	OpenMP	TBB
1	0.91	0.85	1.56	1.78
2	0.56	0.54	1.03	0.98
4	0.39	0.38	0.61	0.54
8	0.31	030	0.35	0.35
16	0.30	0.27	0.25	0.25
32	0.29	0.26	0.20	0.20
68			0.18	0.19

TABLE IV. PARALLEL TIME USAGE (IN SECONDS) OF SEISMICLAB'S `FX_DECON` DEMO.

Fx_decon					
	Dual-socket server			KNL	
# threads	MATLAB	OpenMP	TBB	OpenMP	TBB
1	2.92	1.99	1.99	3.75	3.72
2	1.76	1.32	1.32	2.61	2.42
4	1.15	1.01	0.99	1.91	1.72
8	0.86	0.85	0.82	1.49	1.40
16	0.86	0.85	0.75	1.28	1.23
32				1.22	1.21
68				1.25	1.24

D. Further Manual Optimisations

A careful reader will notice that the original MATLAB code of the parabolic moveout example (shown in Section III-B) is not efficiently programmed. One major problem is that the `d` matrix is traversed in a row-major fashion, contrary to the underlying column-major data structure (in both MATLAB and Armadillo). The auto-translated C++ code is consequently also inefficient, even though it is much faster than the original MATLAB code (see Table II). Since the auto-translated C++ code has the same readability, it is possible for an experienced programmer to carry out further optimisations. Figure 4 contains an improved code segment that shows the result of such manual optimisations:

It can be seen that the manually optimised C++ code segment in Figure 4 has swapped the `ih`-indexed for-loop with the `ig`-indexed for-loop. Moreover, the `s` matrix and `ts` vector have now become obsolete and thus removed. When possible, the if-test is lifted out of the innermost for-loop, allowing the compiler to do auto-vectorisation. The hand-optimised code also uses two statically allocated arrays: `s_temp` and `H`, both

```
for (it=1; it<=ntau; it++) {
  for (iq=1; iq<=nq; iq++) {
    time = tau(it-1)+q(iq-1)*arma::square(h/hmax) ;
    memset(s_temp, 0, sizeof(s_temp));
    s2 = 0.;

    for (ih = 1; ih <= nh; ih++) {
       double is_start_double = time(ih - 1) / dt ;
       int is_start = std::floor(is_start_double);
       a = is_start_double - is_start;

       if (is_start-L >= 1 && is_start+L <= nt) {
           for (ig = -(L); ig <= L; ig++) {
               il = is_start + ig;
               ss = ((1.- a)*d(il-1, ih-1) + a*d(il, ih-1))*H[ig + L];
               s2 += ss*ss;
               s_temp[ig + L] += ss;
           }
       }
       else {
           for (ig = -(L); ig <= L; ig++) {
               il = is_start + ig;
               if (il >= 1 && il < nt) {
                 ss = ((1.- a)*d(il-1, ih-1) + a*d(il, ih-1))*H[ig + L];
                 s2 += ss*ss;
                 s_temp[ig + L] += ss;
               }
           }
       }
    }
    s1 = 0;
    for (int i = 0; i < _countof(s_temp); ++i)
       s1 += s_temp[i]*s_temp[i] ;
    S(it-1, iq-1) = s1-s2 ;
  }
}
```

Figure 4. The further improved computational C++ kernel of the parabolic moveout example after manual optimisations.

of length `2*L+1`, where the latter replaces the unnecessary `H` matrix in the original MATLAB code and the auto-translated C++ code.

On a single core, the hand-optimised C++ code runs more than 5 times faster on both the Sandy Bridge CPU and the KNL Xeon Phi processor, as shown in Table V. Although some of the manual optimisations are also applicable to the original MATLAB code, the resulting performance gain is smaller because MATLAB is not a compiled language. Table V details the parallel performance of the hand-optimised C++ code. It remains to be investigated why the hand-optimised OpenMP version runs slower than the TBB counterpart on the KNL Xeon Phi processor (unless all the 68 cores are used).

IV. RELATED WORK

To our knowledge, with respect to automated MATLAB-to-C/C++ code translation, the only existing tools are MATLAB Coder [11] and MATISSE [12]. The former is MATLAB's commercial product and makes use of GUI-supported directives to address variable types and shapes, whereas the latter relies on an aspect-oriented programming language (LARA) for initialising variables and specifying their types and shapes. Both tools are thus, to a certain extent, invasive to the original MATLAB code. Moreover, MATISSE does not support parallelisation in the translated C code.

Compared with [7], the *m2cpp* translator discussed in the present paper has been considerably enhanced. For example, *m2cpp*'s preprocessor is now capable of automatically identifying the type of variables used in the input MATLAB code. Moreover, MATLAB functions that have multiple return values can now be handled by *m2cpp*. A very important new feature of *m2cpp* is its capability of adopting multiple threads to parallelise the independent iterations of a designated for-loop, with help of either OpenMP or Intel TBB. The responsibility of ensuring iteration independency lies with the user, who labels the designated for-loops of multi-threading by `%#PARFOR` in the MATLAB source. With respect to performance study, the present paper has included detailed time measurements of both original MATLAB codes and auto-translated C++ codes, using different core counts on a two-socket multicore CPU server and one second-generation Xeon Phi processor. An example of further manual optimisations of auto-translated C++ code has also been provided to show the readability and traceability of *m2cpp* output.

V. CONCLUSION

Indeed, as the authors of [13] have pointed out, translating MATLAB code to the C/C++ counterpart should be the last option for speeding up MATLAB programs. However, when efficient serial programming practices in the MATLAB context are insufficient or even not applicable, code translation can be the remedy. The four examples from SeismicLab show that the auto-translated Armadillo code in C++ has a clear performance

TABLE V. TIME USAGE COMPARISON BETWEEN ORIGINAL/AUTO-TRANSLATED AND HAND-OPTIMISED CODES FOR THE `PARABOLIC_MOVEOUT` DEMO.

Serial performance	MATLAB (on server)	C++ (on server)		C++ (on KNL)	
Original/auto-translated	261.7	59.5		133.2	
Hand-Optimised	119.1	10.8		26.5	
Parallel performance	N/A	OpenMP	TBB	OpenMP	TBB
2 threads		5.64	5.88	24.52	13.70
4 threads		2.97	3.07	12.79	7.00
8 threads		1.68	1.72	6.64	4.18
16 threads		1.03	1.09	3.67	2.46
32 threads		0.87	0.83	2.15	1.39
68 threads				1.24	1.17

advantage over the MATLAB counterpart, except when the computational core of a MATLAB code already internally uses multi-threaded and highly optimised math libraries such as Intel's MKL. The automated *m2cpp* translator is not only 100% non-invasive for serial MATLAB code, but also retains readability of the resulting C++ code, giving rise to traceability of every algorithmic structure and detail. This in turn allows further manual code optimisations if needed.

Applying *m2cpp* to more real-world examples will be the best way to uncover new limitations and/or inefficiencies of the MATLAB-to-C++ translator, thereby prompting further improvements of *m2cpp*. We thus hope that the open-source software of *m2cpp* [14] will encourage more testing, especially among industrial users. A future research topic that concerns parallelising *m2cpp*-translated C++ code, in addition to the currently adopted data-parallel approach, is how to automatically identify independent tasks in the input MATLAB code and thereafter insert task-parallel execution in the auto-translated C++ code.

ACKNOWLEDGMENT

Dr. Jonathan Feinberg is acknowledged for his important contributions to an earlier version of the MATLAB-to-Armadillo translator. The translator was developed within the EMC^2 project [15] – *Embedded multi-core systems for mixed criticality applications in dynamic and changeable real-time environments*. The research and development work has received funding from Research Council of Norway and ARTEMIS Joint Undertaking (JU) under grant agreement No. 621429.

REFERENCES

[1] H. Inoue and T. Nakatani, "Performance of multi-process and multi-thread processing on multi-core SMT processors," in 2010 IEEE International Symposium on Workload Characterization (IISWC), Dec. 2010, pp. 1–10.

[2] C. Sanderson, "Armadillo: An Open Source C++ Linear Algebra Library for Fast Prototyping and Computationally Intensive Experiments," NICTA, Tech. Rep., Oct. 2010.

[3] C. Sanderson and R. Curtin, "Armadillo: a template-based C++ library for linear algebra," The Journal of Open Source Software, vol. 1, no. 2, 2016, p. 26.

[4] G. Sharma and J. Martin, "MATLAB®: A language for parallel computing," International Journal of Parallel Programming, vol. 37, no. 1, 2009, pp. 3–36.

[5] B. Chapman, G. Jost, and R. van de Pas, Using OpenMP: Portable Shared Memory Parallel Programming. MIT Press, 2007.

[6] J. Reinders, Intel Threading Building Blocks: Outfitting C++ for Multi-core Processor Parallelism. O'Reilly Media, 2007.

[7] G. Y. Paulsen, J. Feinberg, X. Cai, B. Nordmoen, and H. P. Dahle, "Matlab2cpp: A Matlab-to-C++ code translator," in Proceedings of 11th System of Systems Engineering Conference (SoSE), 2016, pp. 1–5.

[8] L. Torczon and K. Cooper, Engineering A Compiler, 2nd ed. Morgan Kaufmann Publishers Inc., 2011.

[9] "ANTLR – ANother Tool for Language Recognition," URL: http://www.antlr.org/ [retrieved: July, 2017].

[10] "SeismicLab: a MATLAB seismic data processing package," URL: http://seismic-lab.physics.ualberta.ca/ [retrieved: July, 2017].

[11] "MATLAB Coder," URL: http://se.mathworks.com/products/matlab-coder/ [retrieved: July, 2017].

[12] J. Bispo and J. M. P. Cardoso, "A MATLAB subset to C compiler targeting embedded systems," Software: Practice and Experience, vol. 47, no. 2, 2017, pp. 249–272.

[13] S. W. Zaranek, B. Chou, G. Sharma, and H. Zarrinkoub, "Accelerating MATLAB algorithms and applications," URL: https://se.mathworks.com/company/newsletters/articles/accelerating-matlab-algorithms-and-applications.html [retrieved: July, 2017].

[14] "Convertion program from Matlab to C++ using Armadillo," URL: https://github.com/emc2norway/m2cpp [retrieved: September, 2017].

[15] "EMC^2 – Embedded Multi-Core systems for Mixed Criticality applications in dynamic and changeable real-time environments," URL: http://www.artemis-emc2.eu [retrieved: July, 2017].

Third-order Time Integration Scheme for Structural Dynamics

Eva Zupan
HSE, Ljubljana, Slovenia
and University of Ljubljana
Faculty of Civil and Geodetic Engineering
Ljubljana, Slovenia
Email: eva.zupan.lj@gmail.com

Dejan Zupan
University of Ljubljana
Faculty of Civil and Geodetic Engineering
Ljubljana, Slovenia
Email: dejan.zupan@fgg.uni-lj.si

***Abstract*—In this paper, we propose a new time integration scheme for rigid and flexible body dynamics, where rotational degrees of freedom are incorporated into the model. To properly consider the multiplicative and non-commutative nature of three-dimensional rotations, the integration scheme is designed in a special way. It employs the representation of rotations with quaternions and quaternion exponential to preserve the orthogonality condition. The scheme is implicit and its accuracy is of the third order. To gain the desired order of the scheme for rotational degrees of freedom, an additional correction function is introduced that compensates the non-commutativity of rotations. The performance of the scheme is demonstrated by several examples.**

Keywords–time integrators; three-dimensional rotations; quaternions; dynamics.

I. INTRODUCTION

Problems in structural dynamics can be very demanding. The differential equations that govern the problem are often stiff and the configuration space usually consists of three-dimensional rotations. Because the spatial rotations are elements of the multiplicative $SO(3)$ group, the configuration space becomes a non-linear manifold. Thus, numerical solution methods need to be specially designed to properly consider non-commutativity and non-additivity of three-dimensional rotations. Simo and Vu-Quoc [1] proposed an adjustment of the implicit Newmark method to treat the spatial rotations. Their method is of second order and can be considered a special case of the methods on Lie groups, later presented by Munthe-Kaas [2]. The crucial idea employed in [1] and [2] is to approximate the update in the tangent space and map it onto the configuration space via an exponential function. However, the non-commutativity of rotations demands the construction of correction functions when higher orders of approximation are desired.

After introducing a basis into the three-dimensional Euclidean space, members of $SO(3)$ group are represented by orthogonal 3×3 matrices. The orthogonality condition introduces six constraints to their components and their treatment is highly important, see e.g., [3]. It seems natural to choose a three-component parametrization of rotations, but no such parametrization is free from singularities. A promising alternative, employed here, is the algebra of quaternions [4]. Quaternions are members of a four dimensional space, therefore a single scalar constraint needs to be satisfied in the quaternion representation of rotations. It was only recently that novel quaternion-based rigid and flexible-body dynamic formulations were proposed, see [5]-[7]. All these approaches treat the unity constraint of rotational quaternions as a member of the governing equations of the problem. This allows the use of standard time integration methods, but increases the computational demands.

In the present paper, we therefore develop a time integration scheme of third-order that is properly adapted to quaternion representation of rotations. Our scheme exactly preserves the unit norm constraint of rotational quaternions following the approach of Munthe-Kaas [2] and Zanna [8] and adopts it to quaternion algebra. The correction function needed to compensate the non-commutativity is derived to introduce an implicit time integration scheme of the third order. The proposed method consists of two implicit stages of second order followed by an explicit third-order step, which allows local error control without any additional computational costs.

The rest of the paper is structured as follows. Section II introduces some primary definitions. In Section III, we describe a novel time integration method for dynamic problems. Numerical examples are presented in Section IV. The paper ends with concluding remarks.

II. PRIMARY DEFINITIONS

Two orthogonal reference frames are introduced (see Figure 1):

(i) a *reference frame* with a reference point $\mathcal{O}$ and a set of fixed orthonormal base vectors $\left\{\vec{g}_1, \vec{g}_2, \vec{g}_3\right\}$, and
(ii) a *body frame* rigidly attached to the body defined by three orthonormal base vectors $\left\{\vec{G}_1(t), \vec{G}_2(t), \vec{G}_3(t)\right\}$.

The body frame is at an arbitrary time, t, uniquely defined by the position vector $\vec{r}(t)$ of its origin and by the rotation between the base vectors $\left\{\vec{g}_1, \vec{g}_2, \vec{g}_3\right\}$ and $\left\{\vec{G}_1(t), \vec{G}_2(t), \vec{G}_3(t)\right\}$. Here, we employ rotational quaternions to parametrize the rotations. Using the algebra of quaternions, the relation between the moving and the fixed basis is written as

$$\vec{G}_i(t) = \widehat{q}(t) \circ \vec{g}_i \circ \widehat{q}^*(t), \qquad i = 1, 2, 3, \tag{1}$$

where $\widehat{q}$ is the rotational quaternion, $\widehat{q}^*$ is the conjugated quaternion, and $(\circ)$ denotes the quaternion product.

The set of quaternions $\mathbb{H}$ is a four-dimensional Euclidean space. Quaternions can be described as the sum of a scalar and a vector: $\widehat{x} = s + \vec{v} = \left(s, \vec{v}\right)$, $s \in \mathbb{R}$, $\vec{v} \in \mathbb{R}^3$. Addition

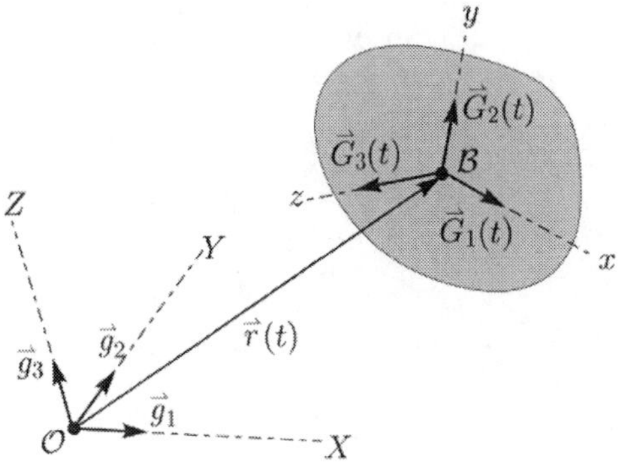

Figure 1. Base vectors.

and scalar multiplication are inherited from $I\!R^4$, while the *quaternion multiplication* is defined as:

$$\widehat{x} \circ \widehat{y} = \left(s\,c - \vec{v} \cdot \vec{w}\right) + \left(c\vec{v} + s\vec{w} + \vec{v} \times \vec{w}\right), \quad (2)$$

where $\widehat{y} = c + \vec{w} \in I\!H$ and $(\cdot)$ and $(\times)$ are the scalar and the cross-vector product, respectively. The quaternion multiplication is associative but it is not commutative, which makes the set of quaternions an associative non-commutative algebra over $I\!R$. In what follows, abstract elements of $I\!R^3$ and $I\!H$ will be replaced by one-column representations and will be denoted by bold face symbols. The additional base vector of quaternion space is taken to be the identity element $\widehat{1} = 1 + \vec{0}$. An arbitrary quaternion, $\widehat{x} = s + \vec{v}$, can thus be expressed with respect to either of the two bases

$$\widehat{x} = s\,\widehat{1} + v_1\vec{g}_1 + v_2\vec{g}_2 + v_3\vec{g}_3 = S\,\widehat{1} + V_1\vec{G}_1 + V_2\vec{G}_2 + V_3\vec{G}_3$$

and the components are gathered in one-column matrices. For a more detailed presentation of the quaternion algebra, the reader is referred to the textbook [4].

The differentiation of quantities with respect to time t is essential for dynamics. To describe the rate of change of the position vector, we introduce

$$\mathbf{v} = \dot{\mathbf{r}}, \quad (3)$$

describing the *velocity* in the global frame. The differentiation of equation (1) with respect to t gives a measure for the rate of change of the local basis:

$$\boldsymbol{\Omega} = 2\widehat{\mathbf{q}}^* \circ \dot{\widehat{\mathbf{q}}}, \quad (4)$$

where $\boldsymbol{\Omega}$ denotes the *angular velocity* with respect to the local basis. Furthermore, we define acceleration as $\mathbf{a} = \dot{\mathbf{v}}$ and angular acceleration as $\boldsymbol{\alpha} = \dot{\boldsymbol{\Omega}}$.

As they are a part of many engineering problems, spatial rotations often need to be reconstructed from the prescribed, measured or assumed angular velocity field, i.e., an efficient solution for equation (4) is desired. For the special case of constant angular velocity, a closed form analytical solution of the initial value problem

$$\dot{\widehat{\mathbf{q}}}(t) = \frac{1}{2}\widehat{\mathbf{q}}(t) \circ \boldsymbol{\Omega}, \qquad \widehat{\mathbf{q}}(t_0) = \widehat{\mathbf{q}}_0, \quad (5)$$

can be found. It reads

$$\widehat{\mathbf{q}}(t) = \widehat{\mathbf{q}}_0 \circ \exp\left(\frac{t}{2}\overline{\boldsymbol{\Omega}}\right), \quad (6)$$

where the *quaternion exponential* exp is defined by infinite power series:

$$\exp(\widehat{\mathbf{x}}) = \sum_{k=1}^{\infty} \frac{\widehat{\mathbf{x}}^k}{1!} = \widehat{\mathbf{1}} + \frac{\widehat{\mathbf{x}}}{1!} + \frac{1}{2!}\widehat{\mathbf{x}} \circ \widehat{\mathbf{x}} + \frac{1}{3!}\widehat{\mathbf{x}} \circ \widehat{\mathbf{x}} \circ \widehat{\mathbf{x}} + ... \quad (7)$$

The result (6) indicates that the exponential map may also be a suitable choice for the approximation of the general solution. We need to point out that, without some additional effort, its direct use results in only second-order approximations of the exact solution. The details are presented in [9].

After we introduce the rotational vector $\boldsymbol{\vartheta} = \vartheta\mathbf{n}$, where ϑ is the angle of rotation and $\mathbf{n}$ denotes the unit vector on the axis of rotation, any rotational quaternion can also be expressed as

$$\widehat{\mathbf{q}}(\boldsymbol{\vartheta}) = \cos\frac{\vartheta}{2} + \sin\frac{\vartheta}{2}\frac{\boldsymbol{\vartheta}}{\vartheta}, \quad (8)$$

which gives a firm physical meaning to its components.

III. Time Discretization

To solve the set of differential equations of a moving body, a third-order integration scheme is proposed. Since the equations we are dealing with are often stiff, we stem from the well known combination of trapezoidal rule and backward differentiation formula (TR-BDF2 method) [10], adopt it to differential equations of the second order and extend it to properly consider the rotational degrees of freedom. The TR-BDF2 scheme consists of three-stages: the first two stages are implicit schemes of second order while the third stage is explicit and of the third order of accuracy. The corresponding Butcher array [10] reads

$$\begin{array}{c|ccc} 0 & 0 & 0 & 0 \\ \tau & \tau/2 & \tau/2 & 0 \\ 1 & w & w & \tau/2 \\ \hline & w & w & \tau/2 \\ \hline & (2-\tau)/6 & (3\tau+2)/6 & \tau/6 \end{array}, \quad (9)$$

where $\tau = 2 - \sqrt{2}$ and $w = \frac{\sqrt{2}}{4}$. The difference between the formulae of third and second order allows the local error control without any additional computational costs.

The scheme (9) is adopted here to solve the equations of dynamic equilibrium. Average velocities and average angular velocities between the two successive times are chosen as the primary iterative unknowns of the scheme. Such a choice is especially important for rotational degrees of freedom since the angular velocities, when expressed with respect to the moving basis, are additive. This property simplifies the linearization and update procedure needed in implicit schemes on non-linear configuration spaces. A detailed description of each stage of the proposed scheme will be presented in the sequel. To indicate that a particular quantity $(\cdot)$ is evaluated at a time t_m we employ the notation: $(\cdot)^{[m]}$.

A. *First stage*

Let us assume that the configuration of a moving body is known at the discrete time t_n. The size of a current time step is denoted by h. The first stage gives the approximation of kinematic quantities at the intermediate time $t_{n+\tau} = t_n + \tau h$. Directly from the trapezoidal rule, we have:

$$\overline{\mathbf{v}} = \frac{\mathbf{v}^{[n]} + \mathbf{v}^{[n+\tau]}}{2} = \frac{\mathbf{r}^{[n+1]} - \mathbf{r}^{[n]}}{\tau h}, \tag{10}$$

which yields

$$\mathbf{r}^{[n+\tau]} = \mathbf{r}^{[n]} + \tau h \overline{\mathbf{v}}.$$

An analogous formula can be used for linear accelerations:

$$\frac{\mathbf{a}^{[n]} + \mathbf{a}^{[n+\tau]}}{2} = \frac{\mathbf{v}^{[n+\tau]} - \mathbf{v}^{[n]}}{\tau h}.$$

The average velocity $\overline{\mathbf{v}}$ is chosen to be the iterative unknown of the scheme while the remaining quantities are expressed with the values at the current time t_n and $\overline{\mathbf{v}}$. This gives

$$\begin{aligned}\mathbf{r}^{[n+\tau]} &= \mathbf{r}^{[n]} + \tau h \overline{\mathbf{v}} \\ \mathbf{v}^{[n+\tau]} &= -\mathbf{v}^{[n]} + 2\overline{\mathbf{v}} \\ \mathbf{a}^{[n+\tau]} &= -\mathbf{a}^{[n]} - \frac{4}{\tau h}\mathbf{v}^{[n]} + \frac{4}{\tau h}\overline{\mathbf{v}}.\end{aligned} \tag{11}$$

A similar approach can be used for rotational degrees of freedom, however the relation between rotational quaternions and angular velocities is based on the result (6) which preserves the configuration space and is second-order accurate. The corresponding scheme then reads

$$\begin{aligned}\widehat{\mathbf{q}}^{[n+\tau]} &= \widehat{\mathbf{q}}^{[n]} \circ \exp\left(\frac{\tau h}{2}\overline{\boldsymbol{\Omega}}\right) \\ \boldsymbol{\Omega}^{[n+\tau]} &= -\boldsymbol{\Omega}^{[n]} + 2\overline{\boldsymbol{\Omega}} \\ \boldsymbol{\alpha}^{[n+\tau]} &= -\boldsymbol{\alpha}^{[n]} - \frac{4}{\tau h}\boldsymbol{\Omega}^{[n]} + \frac{4}{\tau h}\overline{\boldsymbol{\Omega}},\end{aligned} \tag{12}$$

where $\overline{\boldsymbol{\Omega}}$ denotes the average angular velocity vector

$$\overline{\boldsymbol{\Omega}} = \frac{\boldsymbol{\Omega}^{[n]} + \boldsymbol{\Omega}^{[n+\tau]}}{2}, \tag{13}$$

which is taken to be the iterative unknown of the scheme.

Two possible predictors of the first stage seem natural: (i) $\mathbf{v}_0^{[n+\tau]} = \mathbf{v}^{[n]}$ and $\boldsymbol{\Omega}_0^{[n+\tau]} = \boldsymbol{\Omega}^{[n]}$ or (ii) $\mathbf{a}_0^{[n+\tau]} = \mathbf{a}^{[n]}$ and $\boldsymbol{\alpha}_0^{[n+\tau]} = \boldsymbol{\alpha}^{[n]}$. The first one was found unsuitable as it sometimes leads to the instability of long-term numerical calculations. Therefore, the second predictor, based on the accelerations from the previous time step, is used here. The initial guess for the remaining quantities then follows directly from (11)–(12)

B. *Second stage*

The second stage is based on second order approximation at time t_{n+1} using the configuration values at times t_n and $t_{n+\tau}$. The third line of (9) gives:

$$\begin{aligned}\mathbf{r}^{[n+1]} &= \mathbf{r}^{[n]} + h\left(w\mathbf{v}^{[n]} + w\mathbf{v}^{[n+\tau]} + \frac{\tau}{2}\mathbf{v}^{[n+1]}\right) \\ \mathbf{v}^{[n+1]} &= \mathbf{v}^{[n]} + h\left(w\mathbf{a}^{[n]} + w\mathbf{a}^{[n+\tau]} + \frac{\tau}{2}\mathbf{a}^{[n+1]}\right).\end{aligned}$$

We now use the notation

$$\overline{\mathbf{v}} = w\mathbf{v}^{[n]} + w\mathbf{v}^{[n+\tau]} + \frac{\tau}{2}\mathbf{v}^{[n+1]} \tag{14}$$

and treat $\overline{\mathbf{v}}$ as the primary iterative unknown. The second stage expressed with $\overline{\mathbf{v}}$ now reads:

$$\begin{aligned}\mathbf{r}^{[n+1]} &= \mathbf{r}^{[n]} + h\overline{\mathbf{v}} \\ \mathbf{v}^{[n+1]} &= -\frac{2w}{\tau}\left(\mathbf{v}^{[n]} + \mathbf{v}^{[n+\tau]}\right) + \frac{2}{\tau}\overline{\mathbf{v}} \\ \mathbf{a}^{[n+1]} &= -\frac{2w}{\tau}\left(\mathbf{a}^{[n]} + \mathbf{a}^{[n+\tau]}\right) \\ &\quad - \frac{4}{\tau^2 h}\left(\left(w + \frac{\tau}{2}\right)\mathbf{v}^{[n]} + w\mathbf{v}^{[n+\tau]}\right) + \frac{4}{\tau^2 h}\overline{\mathbf{v}}.\end{aligned} \tag{15}$$

Analogous scheme for rotational degrees of freedom is obtained by considering (6):

$$\begin{aligned}\widehat{\mathbf{q}}^{[n+\tau]} &= \widehat{\mathbf{q}}^{[n]} \circ \exp\left(\frac{h}{2}\overline{\boldsymbol{\Omega}}\right) \\ \boldsymbol{\Omega}^{[n+\tau]} &= -\frac{2w}{\tau}\left(\boldsymbol{\Omega}^{[n]} + \boldsymbol{\Omega}^{[n+\tau]}\right) + \frac{2}{\tau}\overline{\boldsymbol{\Omega}} \\ \boldsymbol{\alpha}^{[n+\tau]} &= -\frac{2w}{\tau}\left(\alpha^{[n]} + \alpha^{[n+\tau]}\right) \\ &\quad - \frac{4}{\tau^2 h}\left(\left(w + \frac{\tau}{2}\right)\boldsymbol{\Omega}^{[n]} + w\boldsymbol{\Omega}^{[n+\tau]}\right) + \frac{4}{\tau^2 h}\overline{\boldsymbol{\Omega}},\end{aligned} \tag{16}$$

where

$$\overline{\boldsymbol{\Omega}} = w\boldsymbol{\Omega}^{[n]} + w\boldsymbol{\Omega}^{[n+\tau]} + \frac{\tau}{2}\boldsymbol{\Omega}^{[n+1]}. \tag{17}$$

From the known values at t_n and $t_{n+\tau}$ we can evaluate a better predictor for the second stage. A cubic Hermit interpolation, see, e.g., [11], of velocities and angular velocities trough t_n and $t_{n+\tau}$ yields

$$\begin{aligned}\mathbf{v}_0^{[n+1]} &= \mathbf{v}^{[n]} + \frac{2-3\tau}{\tau^3}\left(\mathbf{v}^{[n]} - \mathbf{v}^{[n+\tau]}\right) \\ &\quad + \frac{h(1-\tau)}{\tau^2}\left((1-\tau)\mathbf{a}^{[n]} + \mathbf{a}^{[n+\tau]}\right) \\ \boldsymbol{\Omega}_0^{[n+1]} &= \boldsymbol{\Omega}^{[n]} + \frac{2-3\tau}{\tau^3}\left(\boldsymbol{\Omega}^{[n]} - \boldsymbol{\Omega}^{[n+\tau]}\right) \\ &\quad + \frac{h(1-\tau)}{\tau^2}\left((1-\tau)\boldsymbol{\alpha}^{[n]} + \boldsymbol{\alpha}^{[n+\tau]}\right).\end{aligned}$$

C. *Third stage*

Finally, we use an explicit third-order scheme to increase the accuracy of the results at time t_{n+1}. For the position vector, we can directly employ the last line of Butcher's array (9), which gives

$$\mathbf{r}^{[n+1]} = \mathbf{r}^{[n]} + h\left(\frac{1-w}{3}\mathbf{v}^{[n]} + \frac{3w+1}{3}\mathbf{v}^{[n+\tau]} + \frac{\tau}{6}\mathbf{v}^{[n+1]}\right). \tag{18}$$

Analogous formula for rotational degrees of freedom can be written as

$$\begin{aligned}\widehat{\mathbf{q}}^{[n+1]} &= \widehat{\mathbf{q}}^{[n]} \circ \exp\Big(\mathrm{Corr} \\ &\quad + \frac{h}{2}\left(\frac{1-w}{3}\boldsymbol{\Omega}^{[n]} + \frac{3w+1}{3}\boldsymbol{\Omega}^{[n+\tau]} + \frac{\tau}{6}\boldsymbol{\Omega}^{[n+1]}\right)\Big),\end{aligned} \tag{19}$$

where the correction term Corr is needed to gain the third order of accuracy. Thus, the correction term is determined in such a way that (19) agrees with the analytical solution of Eq. (5) up to the third order. After a lenghty derivation and taking into account the analytical solution presented in [9], we get

$$\mathrm{Corr} = \frac{h^2}{48\tau(\tau-1)}\boldsymbol{\Omega}^{[n]} \times \left(\tau^2\boldsymbol{\Omega}^{[n+1]} - \boldsymbol{\Omega}^{[n+\tau]}\right). \tag{20}$$

In contrast to the previous two stages, velocities and angular velocities are left unchanged since their higher order approximation quickly amplifies stiff components of the system and the convergence of the method deteriorates.

IV. Numerical Studies

We will demonstrate the performance of the proposed method on several numerical examples. Quadratic convergence of Newton iteration scheme was achieved in all examples due to consistent linearization of equations with proper consideration of rotational degrees of freedom.

A. *Rotating body under prescribed torque*

In the first set of examples, we consider a rotating rigid body subjected only to the analytically prescribed external torque $\boldsymbol{M}$. Equations of motion are then as follows

$$\mathbf{J}\dot{\boldsymbol{\Omega}} + \boldsymbol{\Omega} \times \mathbf{J}\boldsymbol{\Omega} = \widehat{\mathrm{q}}^* \circ \boldsymbol{M} \circ \widehat{\mathrm{q}}, \tag{21}$$

where $\mathbf{J}$ is the inertia matrix. When equation (21) is evaluated at discrete time t_{n+1} and the proposed time discretization is taken into account, the average velocities and angular velocities, $\overline{\mathbf{v}}$ and $\overline{\boldsymbol{\Omega}}$, become the only unknowns of the problem. The obtained time-discrete equations are non-linear and are therefore solved iteratively.

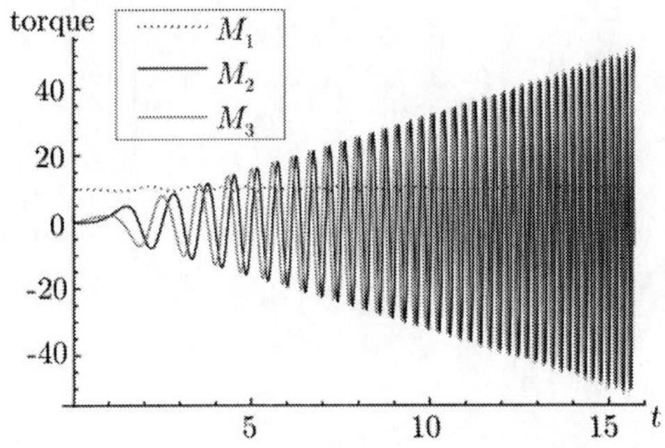

Figure 2. The torque applied to the rigid body. Load case (i).

We base this test on the assumed analytical field of rotations, i.e., the components of the rotational vector are known analytical functions of time. From (5), (8) and (21) we obtain the analytical expression for the applied torque $\boldsymbol{M}$ and the initial values $\widehat{\mathrm{q}}_0 = \widehat{\mathrm{q}}(0)$ and $\boldsymbol{\Omega}^{[0]} = \boldsymbol{\Omega}(0)$. We employed Mathematica [12] for these symbolic manipulations. From the numerically obtained rotational quaternions the discrete numerical solution in terms of rotational vectors is evaluated using the Spurrier algorithm [13]. Numerical results are then compared to the exact ones.

Two cases are considered for which the rotational vectors are: (i) the quadratic function: $\boldsymbol{\vartheta}(t) = \left[t^2, 0, t/5\right]^T$ and (ii) the harmonic function: $\boldsymbol{\vartheta}(t) = \left[t + \sin(t), 0, \cos(t)\right]^T$ of time. The inertia tensor with respect to the principal axes of the rotating body was taken to be $\mathbf{J} = \mathrm{diag}(5, 5, 1)$. The results were obtained on the time interval $[0, 5\pi]$ using the present method and in the field of structural dynamics widely used Newmark algorithm for $SO(3)$ by Simo and Vu-Quoc [1]. The absolute errors of the norm of rotational vector, i.e., the absolute errors of the angle of rotation are presented and compared.

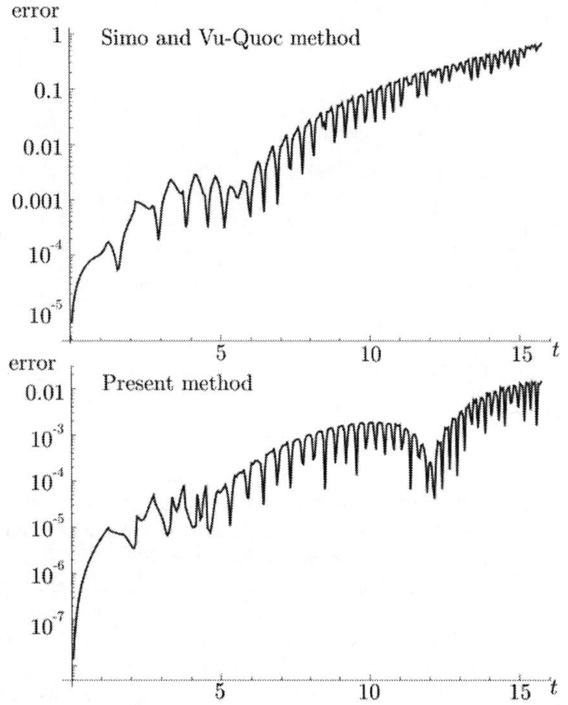

Figure 3. Load case (i). Absolute error of the angle of rotation for the time step $h = 0.05$.

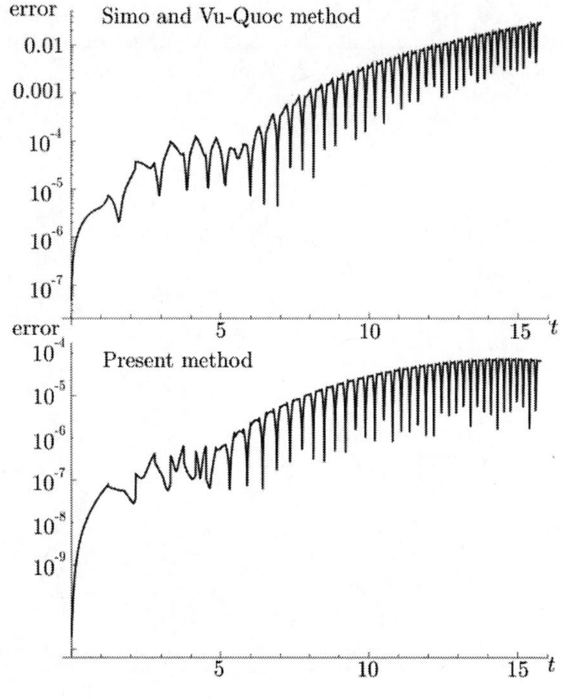

Figure 4. Load case (i). Absolute error of the angle of rotation for the time step $h = 0.01$.

The applied torque for the first load case is presented in Figure 2. The magnitude of the torque is increasing with time

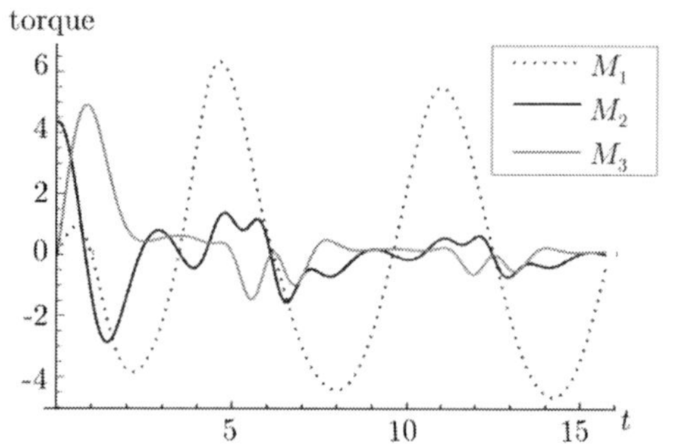

Figure 5. The torque applied to the rigid body. Load case (ii).

and oscilating with increasing frequency, which makes this example quite challenging. For the longer time step $h = 0.05$, the absolute errors between the exact and numerically obtained angle of rotation are shown in Figure 3. Note that the graphs are presented in the logarithmic scale. The higher order of accuracy of the proposed method is evident. This observation is additionally confirmed when smaller time step $h = 0.01$ is taken, see Figure 4. Again, the proposed method is advantageous compared to the widely used method by Simo and Vu-Quoc [1]. As expected, the absolute error is increasing with time, but the higher order of local accuracy of the proposed method results in much smaller global errors.

The applied torque for the second load case is shown in Figure 5. For this load case, the magnitude of the torque is not increasing, but we still cannot avoid the accumulation of the error with large number of time steps.

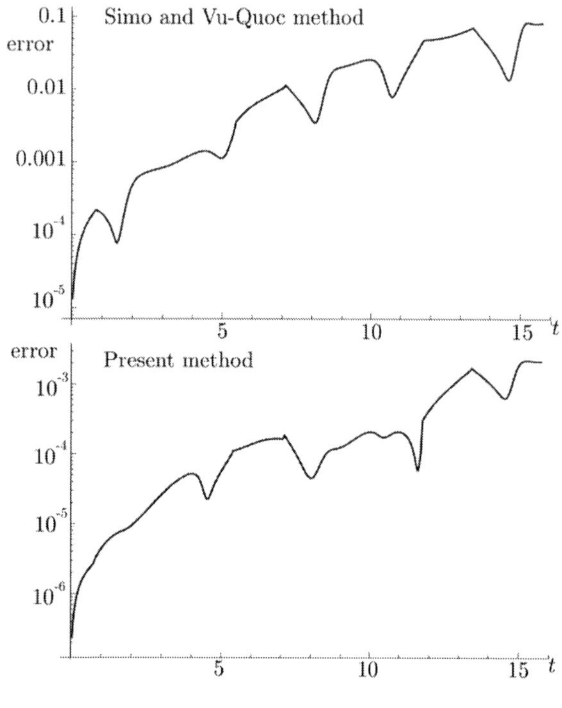

Figure 6. Load case (ii). Absolute error of the angle of rotation for the time step $h = 0.05$.

The results presented in Figure 6 were obtained using time step $h = 0.05$. The maximum absolute error of the second-order method was 0.084, while the proposed method is more accurate with the maximum global error being 0.0022. The accuracy is considerably improved by reducing the time step. When $h = 0.01$, the maximum absolute error of Simo and Vu-Quoc method [1] is 0.0035, while for the present method it is no more than 0.000017.

B. Large deflections of right-angle cantilever

This classical benchmark problem for frame-like structures was introduced by Simo and Vu-Quoc [1]. A right-angle cantilever beam is subjected to a triangular pulse out-of-plane load at the elbow, see Figure 7. After the removal of the external force, the cantilever undergoes free vibrations. Each part of the cantilever is dicretized with five third-order beam elements. Details on the finite elements used are presented in [14]. Both time integrators are employed to obtain the solution. A dynamic response of the cantilever involves very large magnitudes of displacements and rotations together with finite strains. The centroidal mass-inertia matrix of the cross-section is diagonal: $\mathbf{J}_\rho = \text{diag}[\ 20 \quad 10 \quad 10\ ]$.

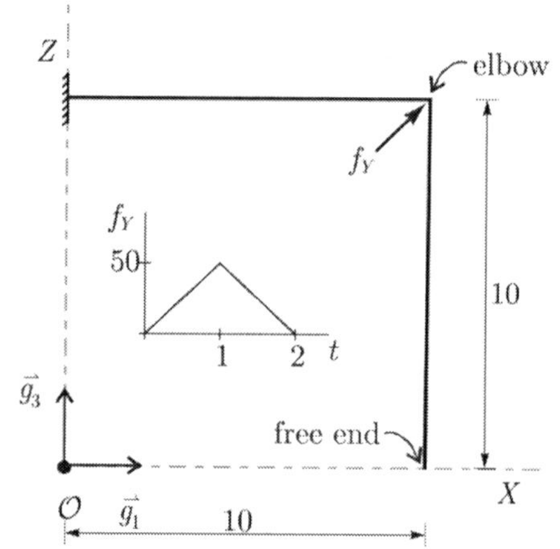

Figure 7. The right-angle cantilever subjected to out-of-plane loading.

The dynamic response of the beam was computed on the time interval $[0, 4]$ with different time steps. Since no analytical solution exists for this problem, the solution obtained with very small time step $h = 0.00025$ was taken as the reference one.

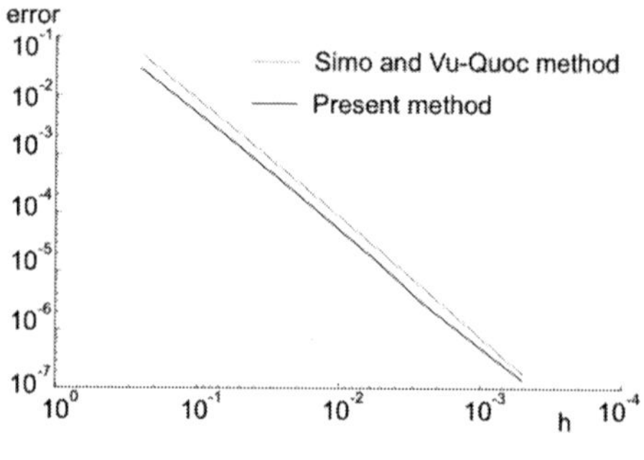

Figure 8. Right-angle cantilever: logarithmic plot of the displacement errors at the elbow.

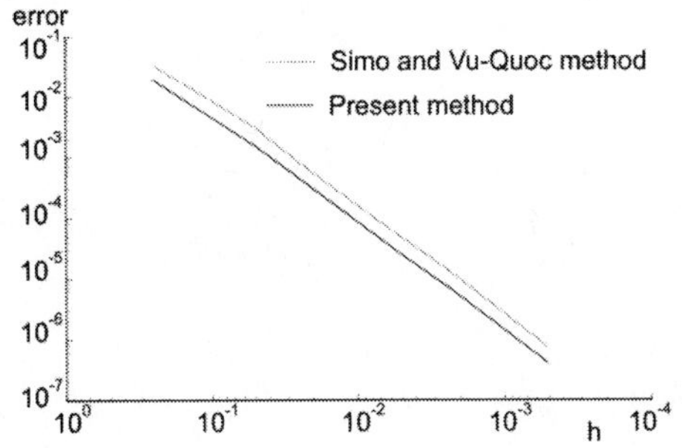

Figure 9. Right-angle cantilever: logarithmic plot of the rotation errors at the elbow.

Figures 8 and 9 present the convergence plots of the results at the elbow. Note that the proposed method gives more accurate results than the scheme by Simo and Vu-Quoc. The difference is evident but not as high as for the rigid body motion. The main reason for this lies in the approximation of strain vectors, which was taken the same for both integrators and limits the benefits of the proposed method.

V. CONCLUSION

We have presented a third order time integrator for rigid and flexible body dynamics. The proposed scheme is consistent with the properties of three-dimensional rotations and allows the rotational degrees of freedom to be treated with the same accuracy as the translational ones. An additional benefit is the local error control without any additional computational demands. To achieve an additional order of accuracy, two implicit and one explicit step are needed in our approach. This means that by doubling the computational costs we gain one order of accuracy and free local error control without any additional computational time needed in contrast to second-order schemes, where local error control demands additional evaluations. The proposed method is thus competitive among implicit methods for rigid body dynamics. The influence of the strain approximation on flexible beam dynamics will be the subject of further research.

ACKNOWLEDGMENT

This work was supported by the Slovenian Research Agency through the research programme P2-0260 and the research project J2-8170. The support is gratefully acknowledged.

REFERENCES

[1] J. C. Simo and L. Vu-Quoc, "On the dynamics in space of rods undergoing large motions - a geometrically exact approach," Comput. Meth. Appl. Mech. Eng., vol. 66, no. 2, 1988, pp. 125–161.

[2] H. Munthe-Kaas, "Runge-Kutta methods on Lie groups," Bit, vol. 38, no. 1, 1998, pp. 92–111.

[3] O. A. Bauchau and L. Trainelli, "The vectorial parameterization of rotation," Nonlinear Dyn., vol. 32, no. 1, 2003, pp. 71–92.

[4] J. P. Ward, Quaternions and Cayley Numbers, Kluwer Academic Publishers, Dordrecht–Boston–London, 1997.

[5] P. Betsch and R. Siebert, "Rigid body dynamics in terms of quaternions: Hamiltonian formulation and conserving numerical integration," Int. J. Numer. Methods Eng., vol. 79, no. 4, 2009, pp. 444–473.

[6] H. Lang, J. Linn, and M. Arnold, "Multi-body dynamics simulation of geometrically exact Cosserat rods," Multibody Syst. Dyn., vol. 25, no. 3, 2011, pp. 285–312.

[7] E. Zupan, M. Saje, and D. Zupan, "Dynamics of spatial beams in quaternion description based on the Newmark integration scheme," Comput. Mech., vol. 51, no. 1, 2013, pp. 47–64.

[8] A. Zanna, "Collocation and relaxed collocation for the FER and the Magnus expansions," SIAM J. Numer. Anal., vol. 36, no. 4, 1999, pp. 1145–1182.

[9] E. Zupan and D. Zupan, "On higher order integration of angular velocities using quaternions," Mech. Res. Commun., vol. 55, 2014, pp. 77–85.

[10] M. E. Hosea and L. F. Shampine, "Analysis and implementation of TR-BDF2," Appl. Numer. Math., vol. 20, no. 1-2, 1996, pp. 21–37.

[11] R. L. Burden, J. D. Faires, Numerical analysis, Brooks/Cole, 1997.

[12] Wolfram Research, Inc., "Mathematica, Version 10.2," 2015, Champaign, Illinois.

[13] R. A. Spurrier, "Comment on singularity-free extraction of a quaternion from a direction-cosine matrix," J. Spacecr. Rockets, vol. 15, no. 4, 1978, p. 255.

[14] E. Zupan and D. Zupan, "Velocity-based approach in non-linear dynamics of three-dimensional beams with enforced kinematic compatibility," Comput. Meth. Appl. Mech. Eng., vol. 310, 2016, pp. 406–428.